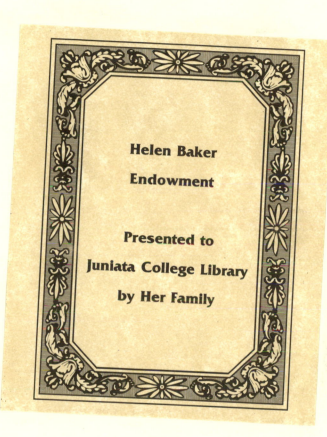

Milošević and Marković

Milošević and Marković

A Lust for Power

SLAVOLJUB DJUKIĆ

Translated by Alex Dubinsky

McGill-Queen's University Press
Montreal & Kingston • London • Ithaca

Legal deposit second quarter 2001
Bibliothèque nationale du Québec

Printed in Canada on acid-free paper

McGill-Queen's University Press acknowledges the
financial support of the Government of Canada through
the Book Publishing Industry Development Program
(BDIDP) for its activities. It also acknowledges the support
of the Canada Council for the Arts for its publishing
program.

Canadian Cataloguing in Publication Data

Djukić, Slavoljub
 Milošević and Marković : a lust for power
 ISBN 0-7735-2216-6
 1. Milošević, Slobodan, 1941– 2. Marković, Mira, 1942–
 3. Yugoslavia – Politics and government – 1992–
 4. Yugoslavia – Politics and government – 1980–1992.
 5. Serbia – Politics and government – 1945–
 6. Presidents – Yugoslavia – Serbia – Biography.
 I. Dubinsky, Alex. II. Title.

 DR2047.M55D59 2001   949.7103'092   C2001-900077-4

Contents

Introduction

Throughout all of Serbia's history no leader has risen to such fame and glory as Slobodan Milošević, or fallen as low only ten years later. At the end of the twentieth century Milošević determined the fate of the Serbs and, to a large extent, that of former Yugoslavia and the Balkans. And similarly, throughout Serbian history no woman has had so much influence on state affairs as Milošević's wife, Professor Mirjana Marković. This book is about them, their regime, and the circumstances in which Serbs lived through their greatest political defeat, isolated and abandoned by almost the entire world.

I first encountered Milošević in 1983 at a meeting of journalists at *Politika*, the leading Serbian daily. There was nothing about him then that indicated the presence of a future national leader, let alone a notorious figure the whole world would have to deal with. In communist regimes, party officials often attended meetings of journalists and commentators. Milošević came to our meeting while he was still a junior, second-rate politician, fulfilling a party assignment. It was his first and only visit to a journalists' meeting, and it ended in a fiasco for him. The culprit was Miroslav Radojčić, *Politika*'s ace international commentator who, after having served two back-to-back terms in London and New York, seemed to have forgotten in which country the meeting was taking place.

Radojčić was irritated by Communist Party officials who presumed they could impose their views on Serbian journalism. He felt they needed to be put in their rightful place and chose to do just that during Milošević's visit. After Milošević's speech, which did not differ from the standard political diatribes, Radojčić spoke out: "Who is this man, and what right does he have to tell us how to do our job?"

Jaws dropped. Some looked at their shoes, others at the ceiling, while the editor-in-chief rolled his eyes in despair. How would the Party comrade react?

Milošević kept his cool and did not react with fury. Only the sudden paleness of his face showed the surprise he felt. The meeting was brought to a hasty close, and we all went our separate ways. Milošević never returned, and none of us imagined what fate would bestow on us in the years to come. Almost overnight Milošević became master of our lives and, among other things, systematically destroyed and humiliated the relatively free Serbian press.

Milošević's rise to power coincided with my leaving active journalism. From then on, for the past twelve years, he has been the focus of my professional interest. Almost all my professional activity over this time has been devoted to the study of the Serbian regime and the life of Slobodan Milošević. During this time, under extremely difficult circumstances, I published four books: *Kako se dogodio vodja* (*How the Leader Emerged*) in 1991, *Izmedju slave i anateme* (*Between Glory and Anathema*) in 1994, *On, ona i mi* (*He, She, and Us*) in 1997, and *Kraj srpske bajke*, the Serbian version of this book, in 1999.

The present book is the first biographical account of Milošević and his wife, Mirjana, to be translated into English from a text written in Serbian by an insider, someone who has followed the events at close quarters and shared in Serbia's fate. It describes ten years of Milošević's rule. The Yugoslav version was published after the arrival of NATO-led troops in Kosovo. Since then the regression in Serbia's society has intensified and, with an explosion of discontent in the fall of 2000, brought Milošević's rule to an end.

Just as the English edition was being prepared for publication, the Serbian political uprising culminated in a gathering of a million people in Belgrade. Serbia finally succeeded in ridding itself of a regime that had brought it down to the lowest levels of social, moral, and economic misery. Fighting for their survival, the people won a historic victory over the Milošović regime and its mindless policies. The description of these events now forms the book's penultimate chapter. Since I have not yet revised the Serbian edition, this English version is the first to tell the complete story of Slobodan Milošević from his ascent to his fall. It represents a sad and gloomy page of Serbian history.

Slavoljub Djukić
Belgrade
15 October 2000

Foreword

In five years in the 1980s Slobodan Milošević rose from being a technocrat of little political importance to the most powerful man in Yugoslavia. The way he used that power led to the destruction of the country. He did not seek the destruction, nor was he the only one responsible for it. But his position as undisputed leader of the Serbs – the largest ethnic group in Yugoslavia – and his ill-conceived policies make him the principal culprit and the one most responsible for the horrors produced by ethnic hatred and ethnic cleansing.

During the 1990s Milošević gained international notoriety and became, if not exactly a household word, a leading contender to head the "Villain of the Decade" list, breathing hard down the neck of Sadam Hussein. He was singled out for vilification and, as is often the case, the devil was painted as even blacker than he actually is, while his adversaries-cum-allies, such as Tudjman of Croatia, Izetbegović of Bosnia, and Hassim Thachi of Kosovo, appeared to be less villainous and were sometimes hailed as heroes simply because they resisted Milošević.

A villain of the Yugoslav drama who has largely escaped attention until recently is Milošević's wife, Mirjana Marković. For a long time she acted behind the scenes, shunning the limelight. Only in the last seven years, since establishing her own political party, has she gone public – and learned to like it. But whether in public or private, she was always Milošević's principal and most trusted adviser. In fact she was more – part of a political symbiosis where she gradually became dominant. More often than not Milošević carried out her wishes and designs, even if it went against his better judgment and the council of his advisers.

The present volume is the first book in English to show the impact of the Milošević–Marković couple *as a team*. A lot has been written about Milošević lately, even in English, but Djukić's is the only book that makes the marriage the point of departure. This is an important difference, for understanding Milošević without understanding his wife, and the special bonds that held them together, is next to impossible. It might not be an exaggeration to say that his enormous and unwavering love for her, together with *her* lust for power, was the unfortunate combination that triggered the tragic events in former Yugoslavia.

Slavoljub Djukić is one of the most respected journalists and political commentators in Yugoslavia. Over the last ten years he has given hundreds of interviews and provided political commentaries and analyses to foreign journalists, politicians, and other interested parties. A knowledgeable western journalist sent to Yugoslavia to cover this or that crisis and/or event would invariably drop in on Djukić to hear his comments and opinions. Regrettably, these were often passed on to the public without attribution. Through this book Djukić finally gets an opportunity to tell his story to the English-speaking public directly. And he has quite a story to tell.

Djukić's book offers an entirely new and different perspective to readers in western countries. Most of what has been written about Milošević so far was written by outsiders looking in. This is a volume written by a Serb who actually had to live through the vagaries of the Milošević–Marković regime. And Djukić was not a sympathizer but a critic! This led to harassment and intimidation, but nothing stopped him. He continued the research about Milošević that uncovered the central role of Marković and culminated in a volume entitled *On, ona i mi* (*He, She, and Us*) published in Belgrade in 1997. The present volume is essentially a translation of *On, ona i mi*, abridged and, of course, updated.

Djukić's book is not a classical biography. It is more a political chronology and a commentary on Milošević's regime: his rise to power, his (ab)use of power and, finally, his downfall. Of course the principal actors are Milošević and Marković, but the setting is far broader. Sometimes this may strain the patience of the reader since, despite my editing of the English version, there are still too many actors. But I felt that patience would be amply rewarded as this broader setting, and the larger number of actors, offer a much better understanding of how the regime actually worked.

Djukić's writing style is a mixture of objective reporting, befitting a chronicler, and the blunt, sometimes passionate, comment of a Serb patriot and intellectual, angered by what has happened to Serbs, Serbia, and Yugoslavia at the hands of Milošević and Marković and equally disturbed by some western responses to Milošević's excessive use of force. I recommend this book to the reader, as I have done to the publisher, believing that this personalized documentary will provide fresh information, insights, and comments not previously available in the West.

Mihailo Crnobrnja, author of *The Yugoslav Drama*

Slobodan Milošević (right) and his best friend and political mentor
Ivan Stambolić attending a Communist Party plenary session in 1985.
Two years later Milošević would use a similar plenary session to
oust Stambolić.

Milošević using his voting card with "Against" written on it to stop Slovene initiatives to reorganize the Yugoslav Federation. The occasion was the extraordinary congress of the Communist Party of Yugoslavia in January of 1990 that marked the beginning of Yugoslavia's end.

Slobodan Milošević, Mirjana Marković, and their son, Marko, in the hall of the Yugoslav Parliament (July 1997). Milošević had just been elected president of Yugoslavia, thus fulfilling his wife's dream that one day he would step into the shoes of President Tito.

Marković greets her husband at the Belgrade airport upon his return from Dayton, Ohio (November 1995). Milošević had every reason to smile: in Dayton he rubbed shoulders with the big boys, and the "Butcher of the Balkans" became "an irreplaceable element of peace."

Milošević in one of his infrequent public addresses (2000). Though an effective speaker in public, on two occasions addressing crowds of over a million people, Milošević preferred to conduct politics in small, informal gatherings of close associates.

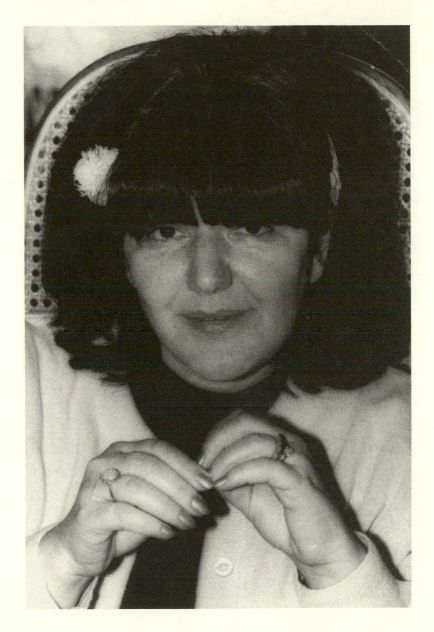

Mirjana Marković in a contemplative pose. She liked to think of herself as the ideologue and the brains of the husband and wife team. Milošević agreed. He was genuinely proud of her PhD and the paltry books she wrote.

Milošević addressing a crowd at the ceremonial opening of a bridge replacing one destroyed by NATO bombs (Fall 1999). He declared victory over NATO and promised unprecedented growth and reconstruction for Yugoslavia.

Milošević, Marković, and their son, Marko, on their way to a voting station in Dedinje, a plush Belgrade residential area. Voting was a bore and democracy despised.

The couple that unsettled the Balkans cast their last vote in September 2000. Milošević lost the elections and tried to manipulate the result but was ultimately forced to yield by tremendous public pressure.

ГОТОВ ЈЕ!

Wanting to see the back of the Balkan Strongman, the student organization Resistence (Otpor) used this poster in the September 2000 presidential elections. The caption reads: "He Is Finished!"

The Socialist Federative Republic of Yugoslavia, 1948–1991

The Federal Republic of Yugoslavia, 1992–2001

Milošević and Marković

1

Fate and Politics

Slobodan Milošević's father was born in Ljevorečki Tuzi, a small, remote village in northern Montenegro where, according to the research of historian Miša Milošević, his ancestors arrived in 1389 shortly after the Battle of Kosovo Polje. Tuzi lies seventeen kilometres from Kolašin at the source of the river Tara and today is more a holiday resort than the isolated village it was in the past. Milošević's relatives are the only family that live in Tuzi year-round. The other residences, about seventy in all, are used mainly in summer, when scattered generations, including my own family, the Djukićs, gather during holidays.

The locals are all related either by blood or marriage, and share the ancestry of an early eighteenth-century warlord, Miloš Markov. Milošević and Radovan Karadžić, the chief Serbian strongmen of the 1990s, didn't meet until the nationalist crisis erupted, but they are also related through Markov, who was the uncle of Karadžić's ancestor, Karadža.

Milošević's relatives cannot recall his last visit. They regret that he has forsaken the land of his forebearers and note that when they used to remind him of his origins in Tuzi, he always replied that he was from Serbia.

Neighbours recall the Miloševićs as titans: big, strong, attractive, and long-lived individuals who were a well-organized and close-knit family and readily made themselves heard throughout the community. Slobodan's grandfather, Simeun, was a local potentate, a thunderbolt of a man who became a captain in the

Montenegrin Army during the First Balkan War. During World War II, the Miloševićs sided with royalist chetniks, but records indicate that a few of them did join the communist partisans.

Milošević's mother, Stanislava, was an aristocratic Montenegrin beauty. Similar personalities and divergent politics led her and her husband, Svetozar, to an unsettled life and early divorce. Stanislava was a schoolteacher and Svetozar a catechist and teacher of Russian and Serbo-Croatian. Acquaintances say they were entertaining but difficult. She was a communist, as devoted to activism as she was to her sons, while he despised communists and didn't get along with his church-going brethren. Svetozar never quite settled anywhere and set himself apart from others by projecting worldly manners and speech and a fine musical sense. Montenegrins value eloquence, and Svetozar displayed his whenever he could, primarily at funerals and in school. Shortly before the outbreak of World War II, he and Stanislava moved to Požarevac, Serbia, where Slobodan was born 20 August 1941.

Mirjana Marković's background is hardly typical. She is an ethnic Serb, and a child of the partisan underground. Her parents never married, but gave their word to the party that they were husband and wife. Her father, Moma Marković, was a partisan commissar who was later proclaimed a national hero, and her mother, Vera Miletić, once helped plan a major partisan assault. Mirjana's uncle, Draža Marković, ranked highly among communist leaders in Serbia; her aunt, Davorjanka Paunović, was a student of literature who became Marshal Tito's personal assistant; she was the love of his life and died young of tuberculosis. Both Mirjana's maternal aunts were radical activists, as was their brother, who died in battle when he was eighteen.

Mirjana was born on 10 July 1942, "in a forest," she says, as enemy forces were closing in on the partisans. Conflicting stories surround the circumstances of her birth; their variance may help clarify subsequent quarrels between her and her family. Though she says she was born in a forest and mentions no witnesses, others say she was born on a communist sympathizer's ranch. And though her father, who had gone to medical school, used to say that he and a peasant midwife delivered her, his wartime journal in which he noted "They tell me I have a baby girl" contradicts such statements.

The child was raised comfortably by her maternal grandparents in Požarevac, in a large house that had belonged to a general who fought under Karadjordje, the founder of Yugoslavia's royal dynasty. Mirjana's grandfather supervised the agricultural holdings of a Belgrade industrialist. She has said that during the war her grandparents told people she was a Montenegrin orphan whom the chetniks were after, and she adds that a notorious chetnik commander once even searched their home while she was hidden in a woodbin in the kitchen. However, the older inhabitants of Požarevac say they all knew who Mirjana's parents were.

Svetozar Milošević left his wife and two sons soon after the war and went back to Montenegro, and Slobodan spent his entire youth in Požarevac with his mother and brother. His high-school years were uneventful. He was solitary and unathletic, always sat in the first row in class, and dressed in white shirts and ties like an official. No one recalls any of the normal fighting, pranks, or disruptive behaviour to which boys of that age are prone, and the impression he gave was of a serious young man. He was well liked by his teachers. "Slobodan was the only one of us they trusted to fetch rifles and grenades we used in our defence classes," recalls a former classmate. Milošević's homeroom teacher noted that he was "intelligent and quick, a useful member of the National Youth Council, who always [helped] his peers."

Milošević's brother, Borislav, is seven years older and temperamentally completely different. He considers himself a Montenegrin, and not only excelled in high school but thoroughly enjoyed life, and effortlessly went on to establish a prominent career. He was Tito's ambassador in Algiers and his brother's ambassador in Moscow, and acted as interpreter between both Tito and Brezhnev and Yeltsin and Milošević. But he also likes to gamble, and has frequently been seen in casinos, seemingly unconcerned abut the effects of such behaviour on his career.

Milošević and Marković were high-school sweethearts, and though they remain close, at the time they were practically glued together. Marković has said that he had a heart of gold and desperately wanted to live in a better world but was also somewhat naive. Be that as it may, he was a shyly conventional young man and married Marković despite himself.

Marković's biographer, Ljiljana Djurović, describes their first encounter:

Snow had fallen. They stood exposed to the wind on a cold winter day, shivering, yet youthfully at ease. It was so touching. They learned that day that they were both exceedingly polite and were well matched. From then on Mirjana feared neither the cold, nor darkness, nor mosquitoes and first days at school, average grades in math or falling from the parallel bars during phys ed. From that point on Slobodan would always stand by her, whether or not she was right. She had found what every woman instinctively seeks in life but rarely encounters.

The couple's backgrounds were far more difficult than the impression given by Marković's fairy-tale biography. These difficulties drew them together. Both of Milošević's parents committed suicide, his father while Slobodan was still in high school. Svetozar Milošević had become a high-school teacher in Titograd, Montenegro's capital. His latter years had been spent in isolation, and for unknown reasons and without leaving a note, he went home to Tuzi one day and committed suicide. One suggestion is that he was driven to this act by a student who took his own life after Svetozar had given him low marks. Neither Stanislava nor their sons attended Svetozar's funeral. Borislav arrived the following day; Slobodan, who was in Russia on a scholastic field trip, never even went to visit his father's grave.

Ten years later, when both of her sons had established careers, Stanislava Milošević hung herself in her home in Požarevac. She didn't leave a note either, but her acquaintances believe that the accumulated pressures and self-sacrifice involved in raising two sons on a teacher's salary drove this high-strung and sensitive woman to such a desperate end. They also say that after her sons and daughters-in-law left Požarevac, she had become somewhat of a recluse.

What's more, Slobodan's maternal aunt Darinka died under suspicious circumstances. According to one account she committed suicide, but her cousins claim that she was the victim of her husband, "a worthless drunkard." And finally, Stanislava's brother, a general, was found dead in his bath. His friends doubt he actually committed suicide because the weapon found next to his body, a silencer-equipped pistol, was traced to secret police in Zagreb.

As for Marković, her mother, Vera Miletić was tortured by police during the war and accused of betraying her comrades. Accounts of her end vary and are largely unsubstantiated, but she was probably executed by a firing squad in September 1944. It is unlikely that she betrayed her comrades, but these distinctions weren't made in former Yugoslavia, and she was portrayed as one of its most notorious traitors. The Germans persecuted her for being a communist, and the communists said she was a traitor. But Vera Miletić would have met an even crueler fate had she lived to find herself on the streets of Belgrade during the liberation. In their revolutionary zeal many young communists brutally murdered their suspect comrades.

Marković speaks of her mother with great affection and has said that "unlike the ambitious and manipulative party members who brought about her torture, she died fighting for truth and justice." During her political ascent Marković adopted her mother's partisan code-name, Mira, and always wore a silk rose in her hair, a socialist emblem worn by Vera. She has often said that she remains faithful to the same "honest communism" for which her mother died.

I got to know Marković's father, Moma, towards the end of his career, while he ran *Borba*, a Yugoslav daily, in the late 1960s, and it was always a pleasure to work for him. Though no longer in a position of great influence, he privately disagreed with the official verdict against Miletić. After the war he had married another Vera, a student of economics who had seen combat with the second proletarian brigade. The couple wanted Mirjana to come and live with them in Belgrade, and Vera told Mirjana's grandfather that the child needed love. But her grandfather was still bitter over having lost his daughter and replied that Mirjana got all the love she needed in his home.

Though Mirjana was never able to accept her father's new family and wasn't close to him, she remained polite until politics began to intrude. She hated having to spend her summers with her father in the Brioni Islands, which she recalls as a luxurious enclave where Tito kept a sumptuous residence and the Yugoslav elites betrayed their true ethic. She says that she could hardly wait to get back to Požarevac.

Her final break with her father and his family occurred during the notorious 8th Plenary Session of the Communist Party of Serbia, when Milošević took over the presidency. Her uncle, Draža Marković, led a faction that opposed Milošević's candidacy, and he later became an outspoken critic of his regime. Moma Marković supported his brother instead of Milošević because he was committed to a more genteel brand of politics. That was enough for his daughter to cut him out of her life. When he died in 1992, his funeral was held in private. The Miloševićs arrived unexpectedly, paid their respects to the deceased, and left without speaking to their relatives.

With six heirs to choose from, Moma Marković left his modest estate to his wife. Mirjana sued, and though her stepmother wrote to tell her that she was open to all possible solutions if Mirjana abandoned her lawsuit, Mirjana did not reply and appealed the court's decision against her. It wasn't the estate that interested her; she announced through her attorney that all of its proceeds would go to charity. What she wanted was revenge, because her father had dared to accept the idea that her mother was a traitor, and because he and his brother had failed to support Milošević. Vera Marković was merely a scapegoat, and though she wouldn't comment further on the matter, she did offer me a startling piece of advice about her stepdaughter: "Be very careful, Comrade Djukić, and take good care of yourself."

2

What Mirjana Marković Wanted

All important matters in Yugoslavia were decided within the confines of the Communist Party, and the key to success was to carefully observe what went on during party meetings and toe the line. Knowing that its avenues would be open to him, Milošević wholeheartedly embraced the party as early as in high school. He would still be volunteering to supervise its elections in the early 1980s when he was running Beobanka, the nation's largest bank.

His fellow students in law school recall him as a "decent comrade" who had a realist's grasp of politics and was discreet, serious, and enthusiastic about party business. He didn't particularly care about school or work enough to excel, but he was a quick study and graduated with high marks. Politics consumed most of his time, and when things needed to be done, he was the man to seek out. In Milošević the party had a loyal and efficient member with "a knack for administration," says a former peer.

Interestingly, during debates held in the faculty of law Milošević was instrumental in the naming of former Yugoslavia. In 1963 during constitutional hearings the leadership wanted the country to be called the Federal Socialist Republic of Yugoslavia. Milošević argued at the university in the presence of numerous eminent politicians and jurists that the nation's socialist character took precedence over its federal one, and that Yugoslavia should therefore become known as the Socialist Federal Republic of Yugoslavia. His argument was convincing and his viewpoint prevailed.

To befriend the right comrade at university was invaluable, and Milošević just happened to befriend Ivan Stambolić, the most prominent member of his generation, at the Belgrade Law School. Stambolić was born into a family of communist peasants. Three of his brothers earned university degrees, and only the fourth remained in their village. Class struggle was never far from their minds. Stambolić's parents wanted him to become an industrial labourer, and he first went to Belgrade and worked as an apprentice, even though his uncle was an important member of the political establishment. He then opted to study law. Stambolić stood at the forefront of a generation of politicians who replaced the partisan old guard. He was an able politician and his rise was uneventful. He was ambitious but also accomodating. Confrontations weren't his style; he was patient and gathered support from many younger, sophisticated politicians as well as the press. He also befriended many liberals, as long as they didn't question Yugoslavia's communist future.

After university, Milošević was recruited by the Yugoslav Army (JNA) officer corps. His academic marks were high, but his physical condition and military preparedness were debatable. His delicate health had excused him from physical education, and he only had a mark of 70 per cent in pre-military training. His former classmates maintain that he never ran and never lifted anything heavier than a spoon.

By the time he and Marković married, both their careers were showing promise. She held a degree in sociology, and was a party activist and the daughter of a ranking official and national hero. She was attracted to the performing arts, and though she often says she regrets not studying drama, her dramatic inclinations emerged later, when she entered politics.

The couple's relationship was intense, so much so that by their own admission it was unbearable for them to be apart. Prior to Milošević's recruitment, the only times they were separated were during summer breaks when Marković went to Brioni with her father. She once showed a friend some letters she and Milošević had exchanged, which she had solemnly preserved in floral-print wrapping paper, an important detail if we are to understand the depth of their bond.

In the autumn of 1968 Marković and a cousin were strolling along the main square in Zadar on the Adriatic coast when they came upon a storefront in which the most prominent item was Tito's portrait. Marković stared at it for a while, then turned to her cousin and whispered, "That's where my Slobo's picture will be one day." Her cousin was startled. For Marković to have cast her young husband, a nobody, as the successor of Tito, the global leader, father, "past, present, and future" of the new Yugoslavia, was completely unexpected. "Do you mean," she enquired, "that Slobodan will one day become president of Yugoslavia?"

"This is how Slobo's picture will sit one day, in a storefront display," Marković replied. To her it seemed self-evident.

On 4 May 1980 at 4:10 P.M., Bora Mirković, the director of Radio and Television Belgrade (RTB), called and told me to go at once to my office. When I arrived, I gravitated by force of habit to the telex machines. Alongside a machine wired to Tanjug, the Yugoslav press agency, was another connected to the Daily Telex Service, our unofficial and not quite legal source. Even though other Yugoslav newspapers were connected to the service, it was officially intended for intra-governmental use. It was a nuisance, because it was used to inform politicians about unorthodox attitudes in the press, but it came in handy to reporters in that it provided reliable information we couldn't otherwise access. During the four months while Tito lay dying in Ljubljana, the service had provided us with confidential medical reports. Now, his doctors were announcing his death.

The two or three months that followed were anxious times, yet they also served to embolden us. The new leadership acted confidently and, contrary to other communist regimes where each change in leadership called into question entire bureaucratic departments, the Yugoslav administration was ready to assume Tito's functions. Preparations began during the early 1970s, and by the time Tito became ill, all administrative power had effectively been transferred to the oligarchic bureaucracies in each of the country's republics and autonomous provinces.

Tito's authority had never been called into question, and as long as he lived Yugoslavia's government remained centralized.

But in order to ensure that no Yugoslav leader would ever again wield the full range of Tito's powers, plans were made for a collective presidency to assume his functions. Under the new system it was possible to know who would be Yugoslavia's president years in advance, and in this way power changed hands quietly.

No changes were obvious, but everything changed. The political elites, JNA, police, and media all appeared stable but, since Tito's powers had been redistributed among local fiefdoms, there was no longer any true central government. Attitudes became extremely lax and, though the government survived, a storm was in the making.

Kosovar Albanians wanted their own republic, the Serbian minority there was upset, and dissident intellectuals were growing less tolerant of restrictions on civil liberties. Aleksandar Ranković had run the state security apparatus for many years and, although he had fallen out of favour during the mid-1960s, his funeral turned into a massive demonstration. After seventeen years of quiet retirement, in political terms he was already dead and buried and his one-time leadership of Yugoslavia's security apparatus couldn't account for the presence of about 100,000 Serbs at his funeral. But many felt that while Ranković was in charge, the Albanians had kept quiet, and as the procession made its way through the streets of Belgrade, his nickname was chanted by thousands.

3

Your Comrade's Embrace

Milošević's friendship with Stambolić turned into a formidable alliance. Stambolić led the way and made sure that Milošević was systematically promoted. First, Milošević succeeded him at Tehnogas, the Serbian gas utility. In 1982, when Stambolić became president of the Communist Party of Belgrade, Milošević was made a member of the Serbian Party leadership. While Stambolić was president of Serbia, Milošević became the head of the nation's largest bank, and in 1984, when Stambolić was nominated to become president of the Communist Party of Serbia, he recommended that Milošević succeed him as president of the Belgrade Party.

Belgrade was the centre of Yugoslavia's opposition, to the extent that Tito had rarely appeared in public without railing at the "Belgrade underground." The Serbian leadership required that the president of Belgrade's Communist Party be highly experienced, firm, and dependable. Milošević was perfectly suited for the job.

He might have surprised everyone and encouraged the liberalization that was afoot. He was a worldly young technocrat, the political vise had loosened when Tito died, there was a thaw in Yugoslav–Soviet relations, and Belgrade was endowed with the nation's most sophisticated press. For a courageous and liberal-minded man, it might have been an auspicious moment. But the party's influence was flagging and the bureaucracy was keen for a revival; Milošević felt that a restored faith in communism and corresponding alliances with key figures in Serbian government would serve his career best. Much to the delight of the Serbian bureaucracy, he confronted and subdued the liberals.

His first move was to secure support from the media, beginning with *Politika*, Belgrade's most influential newspaper. Earlier, the leadership had dealt with the press exclusively through its managing editors, many of whom were brilliant, highly capable individuals who frequently put their careers at risk in order to further their profession's ideals. But Milošević developed a more efficient way of dealing with the press. Instead of issuing directives and fines through his leadership committee whenever unorthodox positions were taken, he relied on dogmatic reporters and others who were easily bribed. His "watchdog committee" thus had no reason to complain or, indeed, to take action. His zealous journalist supporters, certainly more familiar with editorial-room politics than any committee, descended on their liberal peers like locusts.

Similar events occurred throughout government, and officials began to prove their orthodoxy by curtailing civil liberties. When, for example, liberals in the Serbian leadership approved the publication of works by Slobodan Jovanović, the president of the royalist government-in-exile during World War II, Milošević protested. "Let me assure you that Slobodan Jovanović, a criminal of war, will never get by in Belgrade," he announced, adding that whoever wished to read Jovanović could go "rummage through an antique shop." Yet only six years later, during the height of Milošević's nationalist frenzy, a complete reversal occurred; *Politika*'s prestigious "excellence in journalism" award was named after Slobodan Jovanović.

Milošević's first major victory occurred during what was known as the "return to Marxism." There had been an uproar against the content and quality of Marxist education, and the necessity for reform was even expressed during meetings of the leadership. The greatest resistance to reform came from universities, in particular from Belgrade University faculty members led by Mirjana Marković. On 17 July 1985 the reformers lost during a tempestuous meeting of the Serbian Party. Milošević challenged them to "wash their hands of socialism and depart from the central committee and all of its forums." It was a major setback for the party's liberal wing, and Milošević's standing among the reactionaries soared.

He then moved to take control of the party. Having precisely gauged his political capital, he formulated a strategy that virtually guaranteed success: he would assure officials that their jobs were secure, and gather to his side virtually all the influential politicians, including his good friend Ivan Stambolić, the Serbian president. The old guard was delighted that good old Slobo, a "true Communist," was on their side.

Shuffles among the Serbian leadership had become the norm, and it was soon time for Stambolić to relinquish the Serbian presidency. He and the old guard needed to appoint a successor, and on 26 January 1986 their decision was voiced by one of Tito's old generals, Nikola Ljubičić, a national hero and former minister of defence. "Slobodan is committed to our struggle against nationalism, and will oppose the liberals in Belgrade," he said. "Slobodan is a great foe of counter-revolution, and I wish to see activism such as his carried on with yet greater intensity."

Milošević's bid for the presidency was hotly contested. There were eight candidates in all and, had Stambolić let more of the candidates present themselves, Milošević's support would have been diluted. But Stambolić wanted to promote his friend's career; Milošević won by a narrow margin. He arrived at the election's venue in downtown Belgrade walking with a crutch, with one of his legs in a cast. Rumour had it that he had injured himself skiing, but he had in fact slipped on a floor awash with beer during Stambolić's farewell party. Arriving in the same convention hall where in a few years he would be welcomed by standing ovations, Milošević was met with only weak applause. When the Central Committee, of which he would later become president, made its choices, he barely made the cut. He registered only 1,281 votes out of a possible 1,354, very low by Communist standards and definitely showing that he was not the most popular among his peers.

After the vote, Stambolić and Milošević sat in a café, recapitulating. They were exhausted but also invigorated by their mutual victory. When Dragiša Pavlović joined them, the future Serbian president and the presidents of the Serbian and Belgrade Communist Parties were reunited. Though problems were not yet apparent, those were to be their last enjoyable moments together.

During the mid-1980s, when members of the old guard had either departed or no longer had much influence, Ivan Stambolić had become the uncontested leader of a new political generation. As Stambolić's follower, Milošević was able to count on the support of his peers, none of whom thought he would dare to challenge Stambolić. But Milošević felt there was no need to remain subordinate, and in any case would not allow a friendship to interfere with the progress of his career.

Marković stirred his ambitions, wrote his speeches, and turned him against Stambolić. Together they gathered support among reactionaries Stambolić had marginalized, and fostered dissent that turned bellicose during the spring of 1987. Earlier, Marković had indicated what was in store for Stambolić. She and Milošević were in their apartment, welcoming in the New Year with their allies. During a lull in festivities, she turned to her husband and said, "Slobo, Ivan's messing up. Something has got to be done."

Yugoslavia's breakup became imminent in the autumn of 1986, when a blatantly nationalistic memorandum was circulated by the Serbian Academy of Arts and Sciences. Officially, the memorandum was intended to circulate within the Serbian leadership, but it was leaked to the press. It spoke of "anti-bureaucratic revolution" and "greater Serbia," and implied war. Couched in propagandistic rather than academic terms, it was a hodgepodge of nationalist and popular gripes against the Titoist regime, obviously written by individuals who had no clear concept of Yugoslavia's future.

A short section on cultural, political, and economic discrimination against Serbia drew nationwide concern. It referred to a well-known, if unofficial, policy that assumed that a weak Serbia guaranteed the survival of the Yugoslav federation. The academicians accused Croatia and Slovenia of collusion against Serbia, stating that the exploitation of Serbia's wealth that had begun during the Yugoslav monarchy had actually increased during the Tito era. Soon the other republics were making abundant use of its inflammatory contents, which were taken as evidence of Serbia's expansionism.

Usually even the slightest hint of nationalism was countered by intense vilification, and Milošević could easily have taken advantage of the memorandum to reinforce his standing as a "true Communist." However, he confronted the academicians only in private, and skilfully avoided discussing his views on the matter during Serbian Party meetings. He decried nationalism during a meeting of the Federal Security Council, where he warned that the memorandum advocated an "extreme nationalism" and prescribed "the breakup of Yugoslavia." He added that Titoism alone couldn't guarantee that Yugoslavia would remain either communist or intact.

In the spring of 1987 Stambolić asked Milošević to meet with a group of ethnic-Albanian officials in Kosovo Field, Kosovo. On 24 April, fifteen thousand Kosovar Serbs and Montenegrins gathered at the meeting's venue. When Milošević's car pulled up, the crowd swelled in his direction, and police strained to hold it back. As he stepped to the entrance, the crowd shouted that the officials he was meeting were thieves and murderers. Wishing to address Milošević, a few people tried to follow him into the building and were beaten by police. Moments later, as the meeting began, a rock shattered a window. Milošević peered out an open window; it was his first encounter with the proverbial masses, and he was obviously shaken. "They're beating us!" people cried.

"No one," he bellowed, "has a right to beat our people!" The crowd began chanting his name, and he went out to address it in unmistakably nationalist terms:

First of all, my friends, I want to tell you that you must stay put. This is your land, these are your homes; these are your fields, your gardens, and your memories. You won't leave your land, will you?

Your lives here are difficult because you are the victims of oppression and injustice. The Serbian and Montenegrin spirit has never given in to hardship; it does not flee in battle, or flag in hard times.

You must stay. Stay for your ancestors, stay for your children. Would you shame your ancestors, and disappoint your children?

There will be no tyranny on this soil ... We will win this battle ... Yugoslavia does not exist without Kosovo. Yugoslavia will disintegrate without Kosovo. Yugoslavia and Serbia will not give it away!

Milošević became a popular hero that day. Scenes of police brutality and people in tears were recorded by a television crew, and what had been a political gut reaction was widely seen as the refreshingly honest courage of a politician speaking out on behalf of an oppressed minority. Milošević then visited the minister of the interior, Dobroslav Ćulafić, and told him that his speech was a tactic for avoiding bloodshed and not a stand against the Serbian police. They departed on friendly terms, Milošević feeling assured that the police wouldn't oppose him.

But in order to continue his ascent, he needed to transcend Serbia's political establishment. Addressing a meeting of the Yugoslav Party leadership as a loyal Titoist, he stated that all citizens needed to be told that nationalism wouldn't be tolerated.

4

The Vampire Ball

Milošević's faction began its assault on the Serbian leadership by attacking Dragiša Pavlović, the president of the Belgrade Party. Pavlović was young, had earned three university degrees, and should have enjoyed a long and fruitful political career. However, he considered that open dialogue was a political weapon and used the press to criticize government policies. It was a huge step forward, and his openness intimated levels of freedom that had previously been unimaginable, but he paid a heavy price.

The clash began with an incident that under normal circumstances wouldn't have drawn much attention. On the eve of Youth Day, 25 May 1997, an unusual issue of *Student* magazine appeared at newsstands. On the cover, in frayed green print on a black background, was a subtle reference to Tito and government corruption: "The Vampire Ball."

While Tito was alive, there had been numerous attempts to shut down *Student*, whose editorial staff was under the tutelage of ideologues at Belgrade University. Their most influential member during the mid-1980s was Mirjana Marković, and she and her peers now warned the editors that they were committing "grievous harm" to their revolutionary heritage.

The campaign against *Student* troubled many members of the press and other liberal intellectuals, who expressed concern in several publications. A storm erupted when the Serbian minister of cultural affairs, Branislav Milošević, criticized the "paranoid and dogmatic" behaviour of party ideologues. A reply appeared the following day in *Politika*, accusing the minister and "others of his ilk" of engaging in anti-Titoist politics.

Though *Politika* mentioned only Branislav Miloševié, it clearly targeted Pavlović and Stambolić, who believed that an isolated incident was being blown out of proportion. Slobodan Miloševié's attitude during the debate shifted. He first questioned Pavlović's patriotism because he was "anti-Tito" and then because he was an "unreliable Serb."

On 3 September 1987 an ethnic-Albanian member of the JNA stormed into a barracks, shot and killed four of his comrades, and wounded six others. The Belgrade press politicized the murders in countless headlines, commentaries, and letters, and the funeral of one of the victims, Srdjan Šimić, turned into a massive demonstration during which Fadil Hodža and Asem Vlasi, the ethnic-Albanian leaders of Kosovo's Communist Party and government, were angrily denounced. Unrelenting bias in the press furthered the impression that the assassin's motives were nationalistic, even though a medical report stated that he was deranged. (He had fired at random, and there were five Muslims, three Croats, one Serb, and a Slovene among his victims.)

Dragiša Pavlović then decried nationalism during a press conference. "Opportunities to solve the crisis in Kosovo are now so entirely remote," he said, "that the slightest mistake, even with the best of intentions, could well turn out to have tragic consequences for Kosovar Serbs and Montenegrins, the people of Serbia, and Yugoslavia's stability." Pavlović didn't specifically accuse anyone, but it was clear that his targets were the Belgrade press and Slobodan Miloševié.

Contrary to the usual practices, Miloševié hadn't been informed of the press conference in advance, but Dušan Mitević, the director of Radio Television Belgrade (RTB), went to his home and told him it would be aired on the evening news. After they watched the report together, Miloševié told Mitević that it was time to act.

Miloševié, Markovié, Dušan Mitević, and the editors of *Politika* and *Ekspres*, Živorad Minović and Slobodan Jovanović, then gathered in Markovié's home in Požarevac. Miloševié suggested that they retaliate with a press conference of their own, but was reminded by Mitević that party members didn't denounce each other in public. They then concluded that the task would be assigned to a journalist, someone who would be honoured by their trust, and could also be blamed if matters took a turn for the worse.

Marković composed the attack, Minović took dictation, and the article appeared under Dragoljub Milanović's byline. Milanović, a former provincial correspondent who carried a firearm to show that he wasn't to be taken lightly, was chosen because he was always eager to please his superiors and was also known for his polemical nature. The article was decisive, and precipitated events that led to Pavlović's ouster. Milanović was soon promoted and became director of Serbian Television, a post in which he remained throughout the 1990s.

Usually, important matters were only brought to the attention of upper echelons of the party hierarchy once their outcome was clear. However, the case against Pavlović was so contentious that forty-nine members of the leadership gathered to attend an extraordinary two-day meeting. Milošević and his allies were well prepared, but the exchanges were heated and the outcome at times uncertain. Pavlović's supporters included virtually all the most powerful members of the Serbian leadership except Nikola Ljubičić, who appeared undecided. Ljubičić no longer wielded the kind of influence he had had while he was minister of defence, but he frequently played up his military connections, and both factions competed for his support.

The debate focused on Pavlović, but Milošević's primary target was Stambolić. Stambolić believed that Milošević wouldn't betray him, even though he was supporting Pavlović, and at one point suggested that they clear up their differences over a cup of coffee. Milošević refused, stating that he didn't wish to "trivialize" the matter by reducing it to a mere personal conflict.

Seeking to protect Pavlović, Stambolić then petitioned the leadership to abandon its proceedings. There was nothing unusual in this, for his rank entitled him to enter such petitions, but he didn't suspect that his gesture would be used against Pavlović and him.

Dušan Mitević then suggested that a complaint accusing Stambolić of abuse of influence be addressed to the leadership, and that it indicate that similar conduct was invariably at the root of all political dissent and conspiracy. He then met with Radoš Smiljković, Mihailo Milojević, and Jagoš Purić, members of the Belgrade leadership. Milojević was hesitant and asked that a short sentence be added to the complaint. Exasperated, Mitević told him that with or without his sentence, they would all be going to prison if Stambolić prevailed.

One hour later, complaint in hand, Milošević announced that he had important news – so important that he appeared to be struggling as he read through it. He then announced that he had verified the complaint's provenance and could vouch for its authenticity. "I must say, I am upset and feel as though I'm being personally attacked," he continued ... "Such problems have never before afflicted our party."

Ivan Stambolić didn't sleep that night, and his driver, Moša, who was aware of his predicament, was surprised that he wasn't arrested. Stambolić's supporters were abandoning him like so many rats leaving a sinking ship, and the police withdrew his security detail. En route to Serbia's parliament, he learned that Milošević, Lazar Mojsov, the president of the Presidency of Yugoslavia, and Boško Krunić, the president of Yugoslavia's Communist Party, were going to attend the Karadžić Festival together. It was ominous news, for the festival was a high-profile event at which politicians traditionally confirmed their alliances. Stambolić's family was terribly upset; police were cruising in front of their apartment, and his wife fainted when she failed to see him during televized coverage of the proceedings. Two neighbours who were doctors revived her.

On 23 September 1987, during the 8th Plenary Session of the Communist Party of Serbia, Milošević, the party's president, was given a mandate to "defend Comrade Tito's character and accomplishments." The speaker, Zoran Sokolović, then enumerated the contents of Milanović's article against Pavlovic, which accused him of opposing Tito's policies and "shaking trust" in the central committee's ability to remain open-minded, particularly with regard to Kosovo.

(Sokolović and his bureaucratic peers were particularly influential in the Yugoslav political scene during the 1980s and 1990s, but they never challenged Milošević, and for this they would be richly rewarded. Sokolović became the secretary of the Serbian Party shortly after Milošević took control of the leadership, and was ultimately appointed minister of police.)

Milošević appeared magnanimous that day. He tolerated democratic debate, allowed television cameras into parliament, and chastized one of Pavlović's over-zealous detractors. He even offered consolation to Ivan Stambolić, stating that he sincerely hoped, and deeply believed, that Stambolić had been framed.

Nikola Ljubičić then recommended that members "not delve too deeply into such matters, for fear of bringing other comrades into the debate." His warning was clear: get rid of Pavlović, or put your own careers at risk.

Stambolić was clearly no longer in charge. Pavlović was a victim, but Stambolić's fall was tragic, for he had not only been Milošević's mentor but also nurtured the careers of most of his detractors. He stoically maintained his composure, and at one point even addressed Milošević in hope that he could still influence him. "I am convinced," he said, "that Comrade Milošević will rise above the others, and demonstrate a higher awareness of the dangers which are represented in faction." Milošević's only response was to ask whether anyone else wished to speak.

The Yugoslav Party leadership attached little significance to the Serbian 8th Plenary Session and when it convened a short time later, the last item on its agenda was Milošević's report. It stated that "in line with Party policies, an important step" had been taken against "selfish opportunism" during the plenary session and that the Serbian Party was "united, and in league with the Serbian people." The report mentioned "individual deviations from policy" rather than the actual rift that had occurred within the party, and the defining characteristic of the plenary session was described as a "clear and open, democratic, and decisive stance toward Serbian nationalism."

In an apparent demonstration of respect, members of the Yugoslav Party leadership then enjoyed a pleasant evening in Belgrade. Milošević was their host, and the event appeared to be a benign celebration of his recent victory. Six months later, Boško Krunić, who had presided during the meeting, would become yet another of Milošević's victims.

The political careers of all of Milošević's opponents during the 8th Plenary Session were finished, and the remaining members of the partisan generation, including Nikola Ljubičić, were then cast aside. Stambolić was pressured to resign and, according to the leadership, "the people" had demanded his resignation. He became president of Yugoslavia's Export-Promotion Bank and continued to speak out against Milošević from time to time, but after his twenty-four-year old daughter died in an automobile accident, he only wanted to live out his days in peace. At her funeral his wife refused to greet Milošević, and he and Stambolić never saw each other again.

Dragiša Pavlović also withdrew from politics. Relinquishing his right to continue receiving a government salary, he went on the dole for eighteen months and died at the age of fifty-three, nine years to the day after he had courageously denounced Serbian nationalism.

5

The Key to the Serbian Soul

The 8th Plenary Session had been a battle between two bitterly opposed factions of the Serbian leadership. Power was at stake, not policy, and ruthlessness had lent Milošević's camp a decisive edge. Milošević now had a powerful base and could easily have democratized his outlook without putting his office at risk. In doing so, he would have endeared himself to the West, but instead he not only held fast to totalitarian communism but also drew nationalism into the equation.

Titoism had been useful to Milošević, but following Tito's death the only ideas that struck a chord in Yugoslav hearts, openly or not, were nationalistic. After World War II, Serbia was divided into three parts: the Republic of Serbia and its two provinces, Vojvodina and Kosovo. The provinces were effectively independent republics within Serbia, and their leaderships tended to aggravate the political situation by siding more frequently with Croatia and Slovenia than with Serbia. The provinces thus became sparks that set fire to Yugoslavia's nationalist powder keg.

The first major revolt of Albanian Kosovars occurred in 1968. On 27 November the Kosovo chief of police called Marko Nikezić, the president of the Serbian Party, and told him there was unrest in Kosovo which threatened to become violent. Demonstrators were invoking Enver Hodža, the president of neighbouring Albania, and called for outright independence from Serbia. "What have you done about it?" Nikezić inquired.

"We tried to disperse them, but didn't succeed. A few of our officers were beaten up."

"Try harder."

"They want to take over the provincial committee headquarters, and police and radio stations."

"You can't let that happen."

"Should we use force?"

Nikezić approved the use of deadly force. He justified his decision during a conversation with me: "My decision surprised the chief of police. Maybe he thought I was sitting here in Belgrade in kid gloves and tails. But I thought if he was already looking to the head of the Serbian Party for instructions, I needed to be direct and take my share of responsibility. I'm firmly for dialogue, but I won't stand for riots. No lynchings, no destruction of property, no breaking in to party headquarters and throwing people out of windows. I knew that if that were allowed to happen, there would have been more victims later."

The following day Nikezić met with Nikola Ljubičić and Tito, who decided to intervene militarily. The operation was conducted under a media blackout but, given Yugoslavia's stability at the time and Tito's prestige, the international community didn't object. (Obviously, the international community's attitude towards Milošević's regime during the recent crisis in Kosovo was crucial in determining its fate.)

There were deaths and countless arrests, but the revolts proved effective. In 1974 the Serbian leadership approved a revision of Yugoslavia's constitution that made Serbia's provinces autonomous units of the federation. It was a considerable step forward in the Albanians' efforts to gain independent statehood for Kosovo, and the Serbian leadership challenged it on that basis in 1977. Tito then acknowledged that there was a problem but he felt that it was important to promote socialist self-determination in the province. Serbia's grievances were silenced until 1986, when the infamous Serbian Academy of Arts and Sciences memorandum appeared.

But there had been further unrest in Kosovo in 1981, the year after Tito died, which provoked a grave crisis in Yugoslavia. Kosovar Albanians were seeking their own republic, and the province's Serbs and Montenegrins, feeling like a minority under a mortal threat, took to the streets and demanded that provincial autonomy be revoked. But Vojvodina's leaders feared losing their coveted positions and wouldn't agree to another revision of the constitution, and Serbia's priority at the time was to maintain order. Furthermore, Slovenia and Croatia felt threatened by Serbia, and the Yugoslav leadership did little to prevent them from defending the autonomy of the Serbian provinces, which encouraged Albanian separatism.

Slovenia's leader, Milan Kučan, has since acknowledged that Slovenia knew that the Albanians were working towards independence, and that they hoped for a Kosovo not only separate but ethnically pure, and planned to cleanse the province of Serbs and Montenegrins. Slovenian nationalists assisted their Albanian counterparts, knowing they would further their own secessionist agenda by helping to weaken Serbia.

Milošević found the key to the Serbian soul in Kosovo but didn't immediately put it to use. Prior to the 8th Plenary Session the Serbian leadership, including Milošević and Stambolić, were united regarding Kosovo, and though they persistently sought constitutional amendments, any stirring of antipathies was cautiously avoided. During leadership meetings Belgrade generally accepted responsibility for the dissatisfaction of Kosovar Serbs and sought to contain their unrest by banning demonstrations.

The protests of Kosovar Serbs and Montenegrins were systematically and often brutally repressed, and by early 1988, they were ready to revolt. All they needed was an ally within Serbian government, and Milošević was the ideal candidate. Having taken a stand in Kosovo, he subsequently endorsed the 1986 memorandum and persuaded the Yugoslav leadership to oust Fadil Hodža, a moderate whose focus had been to maintain peace between the province's ethnic groups. Hodža was an open-minded Albanian leader, a Titoist, partisan, and national hero. As a member of the Yugoslav Party leadership he had favoured autonomy, was opposed to independent statehood, and was careful not to provoke the Serbs. Thanks largely to Hodža, Kosovo Serbs and Albanians were at peace for many years. His ouster was a tremendous loss, and also a victory for Serb nationalists which would have dire consequences.

Throughout the summer and fall of 1988 large gatherings called "rallies for truth" were held throughout Serbia. Also known as the "anti-bureaucratic revolution," the gatherings promoted nationalism and, to a large extent, ethnic hatred. Hundreds of thousands of Serbs regularly deserted their workplaces in order to attend.

Milošević initially opposed the rallies but soon stated that they were "a genuine democratic reaction" to a real threat, and eventually addressed a rally himself. Milošević is below average height and has short, bristling hair; his face is usually covered in dark stubble, and his eyes indicate a resolve that appears to contradict his chubby, juvenile cheeks and narrow lips, pulled down unevenly on the right side of his face. He proceeded to the dais in determined, quasi-military steps, and his speech was clear, fluid, and emotional, consisting of concise sentences and slogans. "We shall triumph," he promised, "regardless of the fact that today, as in the past, Serbia's enemies, both internal and external, are conspiring against us. All nations hold within themselves an eternal flame that heats their passion. For Serbs it is Kosovo, and that is why Kosovo shall remain in Serbia!"

Nationalist intellectuals embraced Milošević, and he in turn prohibited their censure and purged the media, which became devoted to the consolidation of his regime. Serbian nationalism exploded, and Milošević became the most celebrated of Serbian leaders, to the extent that many Serbs felt that if only their forebearers had had a leader like him, the Ottomans would surely have been defeated at Kosovo Polje. His likeness decorated homes, buses, government offices, and cafés throughout Serbia. Candles were lit for him in churches throughout Kosovo.

Social grievances such as low wages, which had plagued the Communists for years, were diverted through nationalism, and Milošević became less and less willing to compromise with the federal government. He incited uprisings in Kosovo, Bosnia and Hercegovina, Vojvodina, and Montenegro, during which thousands of officials were ousted, including Kosovo's last pro-Yugoslav leader, Asem Vlasi. After appeasing an angry mob that had gathered in front of the Serbia's presidential palace demanding Vlasi's arrest, Milošević had Vlasi incarcerated for more than a year under suspicion of having instigated a miners' strike in Kosovo. And in Vojvodina's capital, Novi Sad, angry demonstrators pelted the leadership's headquarters with yoghurt. Fearing that they would be killed, the leaders begged Milošević to intervene. Milošević agreed, but only under the condition that Vojvodina's entire leadership resign.

Confronted by a revival of the Croatian *ustasa* (pro-Nazi) movement which had persecuted them during World War II, Serbs in Croatia also rallied around Milošević.

A sense that Serbs were a slighted people had been awakened. When the Serbian Orthodox Church displayed Czar Lazar's relics throughout its monasteries, Serbs attended in droves and on 28 June 1989 close to a million people gathered to commemorate the 600th anniversary of the Battle of Kosovo Polje. Instead of seeking to calm the situation, Milošević raised the stakes: "We are again in battle," he declared. "It is not an armed battle, but even that cannot be excluded."

Tito was only a distant memory, bones in a political graveyard. On the eve of the global breakdown of communism and Yugoslavia's own collapse, Milovan Vitezović, a Serbian author, expressed feelings shared by many that eventually caused untold misery. "This year will go down in history as the year which saw the birth of our nation," he announced.

The revolt of Kosovo's Serbs had been intended to halt Serb emigration from the province and change Kosovo's constitutional status within Serbia. However, it turned into a political free-for-all in which Serbian nationalism became a source of tremendous concern, both in Yugoslavia and abroad. Tempers flared. The foreign press cast Milošević as a bolshevik who was desperately embracing nationalism in order to prevent the collapse of yet another communist regime, and Serbia became increasingly isolated.

Milošević paid no attention to international opinion. As his hold on power increased, he became less and less inclined to show restraint, which he felt was weak and cowardly. He believed that his talents were suited to the needs of the moment, and his confidence actually grew in proportion to the number of enemies he collected, and the degree to which Serbia became isolated. When Slovenia supported the Albanian miners' strike, Milošević retaliated with economic sanctions. (He would be amply compensated three years later, when Serbia was hit by the international community's drastic embargo.)

Ekspres and the *Evening News* trumpeted Milošević's policies, but *Politika* and Serbian TV adopted a more informative tone. Under the communists, the editors of *Politika* were cautious, unintrusive, and restrained in their support of the leadership. But on the eve of pluralization they were either ousted or disenfranchised by Miloševič, and from then on *Politika* and the press would only serve to consolidate his regime. Jug Grizelj, one of the most outstanding Yugoslav journalists, was scurrilously removed from his post as president of the Serbian Press Association, and *NON*, *Mladost*, and *Student* were all shut down.

Miloševič became extremely powerful, yet he felt a constant need to validate himself by demonstrating his clout, for which Serbs held him in high regard. Nothing seemed to satisfy him, not even toppling the leaders in Priština, Novi Sad, and Titograd.

During a meeting of the presidency of the Yugoslav Party on 17 October 1989, an attempt was made to vote Miloševič out of office, but he and his allies brilliantly argued that any such vote would challenge Serbia's internal sovereignty and therefore compromise Yugoslavia's adherence to democratic centralism. Though Miloševič was in fact intensely opposed to the concept of democratic centralism he was invoking, the issue of sovereignty, later central to Yugoslavia's breakdown, warded off his detractors. Instead a scapegoat was found in the person of Dušan Čkrebič, the Serbian member of the Yugoslav leadership, and attempts were made to oust him as a signal of displeasure with Serbian policy.

As the meeting came to a close, and Miloševič and his allies were preparing to celebrate their victory, Vinko Hafner, one of few pro-Yugoslav Slovenian members of the federal leadership, suddenly arose and grabbed a microphone. Locating Miloševič, he pointed his finger at him and said, "Comrade Slobodan, please consider the path you have embarked upon more carefully. Think it over, Comrade Slobodan."

6

Farewell

The Berlin Wall, emblem of the Cold War, was torn down on 9 November 1989 amid elated nocturnal embraces. A new chapter of European history was opening, and pieces of the former communist Bastille were gathered as souvenirs. In rapid successsion former Warsaw Pact regimes collapsed, and for a short while only Romania appeared to stand fast. However, the Ceucescus' dictatorship ended violently on 25 December 1989. While crowds in Bucharest's main square chanted "Romania, wake up," television cameras bore witness to the Ceucescus' execution. "We lived together and we shall die together," Elena Ceucescu said as she drew her last breath. "We don't want your mercy."

But in Belgrade the Miloševićs became increasingly dogmatic. In an article that appeared in a Marxist academic journal, Mirjana Marković affirmed that socialism was the future of global civilization. The recent collapse of so many European socialist governments were temporary setbacks, according to her, and the true potential of socialism just needed to be tapped: "Based on scholarship, and within a political framework," she wrote, "socialism will easily triumph, and continue on its historical, civilizing path toward the union of free peoples in Communism."

Milošević was riding a tremendous wave of popular support, and increasingly appeared as the sole, uncontested leader of Serbia. He paid no attention to international opinion and acted as though he didn't need advice. His ambitions had grown, and wishing to expand his influence into the rest of the country, he sought to revive Titoism and called for an extraordinary congress of the Communist Party of Yugoslavia. Marković claimed the congress would invigorate the Yugoslav Party, but she also knew that it was a platform upon which her husband could broaden his influence.

They prepared their strategy well in advance and carefully gauged the delegates. Milošević would be supported by Serbia, Vojvodina, and Kosovo (whose delegates he had installed) and could also count on votes from Macedonian, Bosnian, and even Croatian delegates. But the former banker miscalculated. He wasn't Tito, and if a single delegation failed to support him, his bid would fail.

Slovenia represented a major obstacle. The Slovenian leadership had begun to prepare for secession when Tito died. It encouraged Albanian separatism and obstructed all national endeavours that weren't economically advantageous for Slovenia, a policy subsequently denounced in the Serbian Academy's memorandum as the cause of Serbia's weak economy.

In the mid-1980s most Slovenes began to openly resent the way their economy was being drained by the other Yugoslav republics, and nationals from all southern republics were derided as "Bosnians." During basketball games in Ljubljana, Slovenes threatened and insulted visiting Serbian players. "Bosnians go home" appeared in graffiti on containers in Ljubljana's shipping district.

Milošević knew that the Slovenian leadership was against him, yet, increasingly reckless and self-deluded, he believed they could easily be dealt with. He dispatched organizers to Ljubljana to set up rallies, as he had already done in Kosovo, Vojvodina, and Montenegro, but he failed to realize that the leadership and population of Slovenia were of one mind. The rally organizers became a laughing stock in Ljubljana, and only Milan Kučan benefited from their efforts.

Milan Kučan, a former military intelligence officer, had worked for many years in the party leadership in Belgrade, and had built his reputation by opposing Milošević. Both politicians gained from this rivalry and thus became national leaders who would eventually sound Yugoslavia's death knell.

Slovenia was the first Yugoslav republic to allow a non-communist opposition, and communism and Serbian nationalism were put forth as evidence that remaining in Yugoslavia was not in the republic's best interest. The European community welcomed Slovenia's departure from communism, and when the Slovenian leadership arrived in Belgrade to attend Milošević's extraordinary congress, it had European support and was determined to quit Yugoslavia. However, the Slovenes didn't wish it to appear as though they were leaving merely because they were upset by the economic burdens they faced within Yugoslavia but rather because Serbia was a potentially dangerous aggressor. They weren't let down by Milošević and his allies, who, seeking to affirm their dominance, categorically refused to endorse numerous and altogether benign proposals the Slovenes entered during the congress.

Finally Milan Kučan arose from his seat, nodded to the chair, and walked out. The Slovenian delegation followed, some of them in tears. Someone then announced that those who wept were only sorry to give up their "plush seats" in government, and bid them a sarcastic farewell. After a short silence the remaining delegations broke into applause.

The chair then brought the extraordinary congress to a close, stating that it would "resume at a later date." But it never did, and around midnight, as the delegates were leaving, Ante Marković, Yugoslavia's prime minister, tried to reassure the press. "The Communist Party, a failure, has collapsed. So much the better. But Yugoslavia will survive." However, Slovenia's example would soon be followed by Croatia, Bosnia, and Macedonia. The congress had signalled the final defeat of Titoism, the collapse of the Communist Party of Yugoslavia, and the breakdown of the Socialist Federal Republic of Yugoslavia.

Throughout Europe these events were interpreted simply as a struggle between nationalist-communist and democratic elements within Yugoslavia. Serbs were against pluralism, Slovenes and Croats wanted it. The Serbs wanted to remain communist, the Slovenes and Croats didn't. The Slovenes and Croats wanted a loose confederation, Serbs a strong federation under their dominion. Therefore, Kučan and Tudjman were democrats, and Milošević was a bolshevik. These conclusions were bleak and superficial and only served to isolate Serbia at a time when it desperately needed allies.

Milošević is given to performing stunning reversals whenever he is in a bind. Although most Serbs were satisfied with his leadership, many were troubled by his enduring communism. There had already been open elections in Slovenia, Croatia, and Bosnia, but Serbia would only acknowledge a "socialist" or sham pluralism formulated by Mirjana Marković and Mihajlo Marković, a philosopher, former partisan, and dissident during the Tito era. According to Mirjana Marković, parliamentarianism "suits the British, but really isn't appropriate for Serbs."

Milošević claimed in July 1990 that he was abandoning communism and renamed the old party structure the Socialist Party of Serbia. The majority of communists supported the change, most notably Mirjana Marković and General Veljko Kadijević, the minister of defence, who was nevertheless "saddened and perplexed" because he felt the change bore witness to the definitive collapse of Yugoslavia. Milošević wasn't involved in minutiae, but when he saw a draft of the new party program, he asked that his people be given "another look." The draft was found to have incorporated elements of European social democracy, which were subsequently expunged by Mirjana Marković and her Belgrade University allies.

The first Socialist Party congress was held amid much pomp in the main conference room of Belgrade's Sava Centre. The leadership wanted to show that its new party was truly different. Alongside rather confused former communists were well-known personalities, academics, and writers who had long been their enemies, and Tito's portrait was no longer on display. By simply changing its name, Milošević managed to retain the Communist Party's organizational clout and co-opt much of the opposition.

The author Miodrag Bulatović, an absolute wizard with words, addressed the congress:

Not a single heart in Serbia isn't beating a little faster today, not a single citizen isn't filled with emotion. A new party is being created, new and optimistic, popular, undogmatic, honourable, efficient, and acceptable to all. The colour red, an emblem of this new party, does not frighten me. It is not just the colour of communists, but that of an altar clotted with Serbian blood ... the world will notice Serbia again! Serbia! Our glorious land, which even during the most difficult of times has shone among nations.

On 19 November 1990, a month before the first parliamentary elections were held, a new Communist Party was also inaugurated. It was named the Union of Communists – Movement for Yugoslavia, and Mirjana Marković was its chief ideologue. Marković announced that the party's main objective was to ensure a "united Yugoslav homeland and a wealthy, just, and modern socialist state, unlike socialism in the past." About five thousand people gathered, primarily orthodox communists and Yugoslav military leaders and politicians. The JNA quickly endorsed Marković's new party, and Milošević's friend, Veljko Kadijević, the minister of defence, joined its leadership. Marković was clearly in charge but kept a low profile, beyond the reach of reporters and photographic lenses.

Milošević wasn't bothered by his wife's differing views and policy. Thanks to her, he had the communists' support, and they remained convinced that he was in fact their ally. Earlier, when nationalism had threatened the JNA's stability, his communist credentials reassured the military leadership. Subsequently, Marković's party always supported Milošević, and sought to undermine his opponents. In clarifying her politics, Marković told her party's membership that her socialist, Yugoslav credentials were immaculate, "in theory and in practice." When a reporter asked about her and Milošević's separate political affiliations, she replied they weren't "a sign of tolerance, but of emancipation," which had "always been evident" in their marriage.

Milošević's government then pettily obstructed what remained of the opposition by delaying the incorporation of new parties and exploiting all means at its disposal as the incumbent of a totalitarian state. But the opposition was also unconvincing and immature. Its leaders, who once belonged to a cohesive dissident front, were now socialists, monarchists, democrats, or nationalists. They had only two things in common: they despised each other more than they despised Milošević, and they all somehow felt destined to rule Serbia. Milošević had succeeded where even Tito failed, and divided the dissident front.

Most popular among the members of the new opposition was Vuk Drašković, the leader of the chetnik-inspired Serbian Renewal Movement (SRM). Drašković announced during his campaign that Serbs would "cleanse the festering ulcer which gnaws at Serbia's entrails," and warned Muslims that when he came to power, those who attempted to raise a foreign flag over Serbia would have their hands chopped off.

Milošević didn't need to prove his patriotism, for he had clearly united the Serbs, but his opponents frequently challenged him on that front. Their efforts were futile. The media simply presented them as the rowdy, ideologically inconsistent, irascible, and un-reliable collection of individuals they truly were. They posed no threat to Milošević, who was, after all, a highly accomplished politician. Promising there would be peace, he won the election in a landslide, obtaining 3,258,779 votes against Drašković's 821,674. Milošević's Socialist Party won 194 seats, Drašković's SRM 19, the Democratic Union of Vojvodina Magyars 9, the Civic Alliance 9, and the Democratic Party 7.

But Serbs turned against Milošević shortly after his victory. He was obviously still a communist, and he, his government, and two pillars of their support, RTB and *Politika*, became the objects of popular wrath. During rallies Milošević was compared to Stalin, and members of government were denounced as "filthy reds." The rallies were banned, and on 9 March 1991 a violent demon-stration occurred in downtown Belgrade during which an eighteen-year-old student and a police officer were killed. Police brutally attempted to contain the belligerent demonstrators with clubs, water cannons, and tear gas, and the demonstrators retali-ated with rocks and lead pipes. Fire trucks were commandeered, and at one point a young man climbed on top of an armoured vehicle and replaced its mounted gun with a Serbian flag.

From the balcony of the National Theatre leaders of the oppo-sition followed the bloody events. Vuk Drašković played commander-in-chief and, referring to the RTB studios, ordered his troops to "storm the Bastille." Drašković was in a frenzy and probably imagined that events would unfold as they had in Bucharest. However, the RTB studios were well protected. In addition to sandbags, barbed wire, and a cordon of police guard-ing the entrance, there were 200 officers inside, along with 180 armed guards, and militiamen belonging to the so-called National Defence Unit.

Fearing his government would collapse, Milošević called in the army. At 7:30 P.M. after the violence had subsided and most of the demonstrators had withdrawn, tanks rolled onto Belgrade's streets. Suddenly, an idyllic vision of Serbia crashed. Milošević no longer tolerated the rallies, which had outlived their purpose, and

Serbs were contesting his leadership. That night he appeared on television and justified the army's presence in Belgrade: "There is a fragile peace in Belgrade," he said, "and we must oppose chaos and insanity by all means." The rallies, which he had earlier encouraged as "genuine" national celebrations, he now denounced as "treasonous hooliganism," and he remarked that he had "always thought that problems need to be solved in the appropriate forums, and not at rallies."

Mirjana Marković was terribly upset. During a telephone conversation with the Ljubljana press she blamed Vuk Drašković and said the SRM wasn't a "genuine political party" but rather "a gang of thugs. The city is in ruins," she continued. "There were two deaths, store-fronts were demolished, cars were set on fire, and concrete planters ripped out of the ground. It was a madhouse! Half of the demonstrators were drunk, police dogs were killed, and horses were trampled. It was a terrifying, horrible scene to witness, and residents are quite shaken." However, Marković always stands by her husband on important issues, and she supported his decision to call in the army. When a reporter asked how she felt about the tanks, "those terrible machines that lumbered down our streets," she replied that she didn't believe they were terrible machines and was "surprised that a man should think they were."

The demonstration would have been quickly forgotten if students hadn't been involved. The government feared the spontaneous intensity of their protests, and it was difficult to respond with force. They were, after all, Serbia's "children" and couldn't be dismissed as foreign agents. What the government wouldn't allow the opposition – grandstands, public address systems, gatherings downtown tying up traffic – students could get away with. They made three demands: the release from prison of demonstrators, including Vuk Drašković; the ouster of the minister of police and the director of RTB (Mitević); and unimpeded operations of their own broadcasting units, Studio B and Radio B92.

Their demands were all met, and Milošević, who was otherwise not accessible to the public, patiently met with Belgrade University students and faculty. "When will you resign?" one student asked. "Dear comrades," he replied, "as far as the president of the republic is concerned, the constitution determines when he is elected and when he leaves. All I can say is that I will never oppose the amendment of our constitution, and I will never use force to remain in office. This much I can freely say." When another student reminded him of Kosovo, where he had said that no one could beat the Serbian people, he replied that his views hadn't changed. "However," he added, "we must also protect our citizens, regardless of that which you are referring to."

Milošević now had to face the difficult task of firing his loyal friend Dušan Mitević. Mitević knew that his position was untenable even before the students demanded his removal, and he greeted Milošević with a letter of resignation he already had prepared. Milošević indicated that he could remain at his post if he wished, but Mitević knew better. As he left Milošević's office, he was met by a group of anxious officials who barely contained their relief when they learned that he had resigned.

Later, he and Milošević met to reminisce and smooth over their misunderstandings. Milošević gave him a nickel-plated Colt six-shooter, and Mitević, who is known for his composure, replied that he had more enemies than there were bullets. He had encountered other setbacks, but though his political career seemed to be over, he was soon working in a still more important capacity.

Milošević had nimbly extricated himself from a difficult situation. Students were appeased, public opinion was satisfied, and nothing really changed. Mitević was replaced by a sycophant who would turn RTB into a wasteland, and the minister of police was replaced by Zoran Sokolović, Milošević's ideal candidate for the post.

Milošević then decided that a visit to Mount Athos, the cradle of Serbian Orthodoxy, would help restore his popularity. The monks of Hilandar, the monastery he visited, didn't exactly rejoice. In their opinion he was a "communist, the Antichrist, a dictator who had recently used tanks against his people." When he arrived in a police helicopter, most of them withdrew into their cells, not wishing to participate in a desecration of the memory of St Sava, the founder of Serb Orthodoxy. Their prior had already fled to the monastic seat in Kareja, but Milošević ordered the police to bring him back, and when the helicopter returned, landing in the monks' vegetable garden, Milošević stepped forward to greet the prior with a handshake and a quick "hello." He showed no interest in their monastic treasures and passed with his hands clasped behind his back before Serb Orthodoxy's holiest icon.

When the prior told him that the Hilandar brotherhood continuously prayed for their protectress to wash the blood from Belgrade's streets, Milošević replied that "mistakes happen." As soon as he departed, the monks began to scrub away his footprints.

7

Fat Chance!

After Milošević's extraordinary congress, any illusions Yugoslavs might have entertained regarding the stability of their country were shattered. Intense, long-suppressed hatreds were awakened, and the electoral victory of Milošević's nationalistic socialists presaged the country's tragic future. Nationalism replaced communism, and ethnic antipathies were so heightened that it seemed that nothing could prevent disaster. Yugoslavia seemed to have been created for the sole purpose of demonstrating that related peoples couldn't live together in harmony, and the army, flag, and anything Yugoslav became an object of hatred. During a football match in Zagreb's Maksimir Stadium, catcalls drowned out the national anthem, and the last pre-war game between Red Star Belgrade and Dinamo Zagreb turned into a massive brawl. At the entrance to the stadium a plaque was later installed commemorating "All Dinamo fans, for whom the war began on 13 May 1990 in Maksimir Stadium, and who lost their lives for their country."

Charles Simic, an American poet of Serbian extraction, says that a Belgrade friend asked him why he didn't "come home and join in the hatred." Simic knew that his friend was joking, but he was still shocked and replied that although he disliked a few individuals, he hadn't been able to master the hatred of entire nations. "In that case," replied his friend, "you're missing out on the greatest joy there ever was!"

Tito had failed to resolve ethnic discord, but his immediate successors were partisans who had fought for Yugoslavia and were determined to uphold it. However, those who took their place had no such investment in the country, and by 1990 both Yugoslavia and Tito's generation had become irrelevant.

Milošević caught on late, and his adoption of nationalism was incremental. Early on he supported Yugoslav federalism but insisted that Serbia, its provinces, and Montenegro had precedence over the other republics. When Slovenia and Croatia seceded, he conceived of Yugoslavia as Serbia, Bosnia, Macedonia, and Montenegro, as well as Serbian enclaves in Croatia. When that failed, he turned to aggressive nationalism and sought to unite all Serbs within a greater Serbia.

Slovenia had taken advantage of Serb nationalism and the collapse of communism in Eastern Europe as it steadily moved towards secession. In an attempt to force its leadership into submission, Milošević had imposed economic sanctions against the republic in December 1989. Serbia, he declared, was "morally entitled to ignore and humiliate" Slovenia, and when he was warned that Yugoslavia would collapse if Slovenia seceded, his reply was a vulgar "Fat chance," as though he was convinced that Yugoslavia's future was secure in his hands. However, when his attempts to intimidate the Slovenes proved futile, he began to think that Croatia would be easier to deal with once Slovenia had seceded. The Slovenes were free to leave Yugoslavia whenever they wished, he told Gianni de Michelis, the Italian minister of foreign affairs.

Slovenia was fully prepared to secede. The leadership had begun to focus on militarization in the late 1980s and, unbeknownst to the JNA, whose barracks lay on the outskirts of Ljubljana, handheld rocket launchers and other weapons were imported. With 36,000 well-armed soldiers, broad political support from the international community, and an increasingly divided Yugoslav leadership, the Slovenes knew their moment would soon arrive.

There were hopes that Bosnia would remain in Yugoslavia, but on 27 February 1991 its president, Alija Izetbegović, announced that he would sacrifice peace for sovereignty, but not sovereignty for peace. And later, during an Islamic conference in Teheran, he suggested that if his hosts were to help Bosnia, he could guarantee that Sarajevo would become an Islamic capital.

By early March 1991 it became obvious that Slovenia would secede, and Milošević's allies in the Yugoslav presidency tried to impose a state of emergency. However, this was opposed by the Bosnian, Macedonian, Croatian, and Slovenian members, as well as the international community.

Milošević believed that pressure, threats, and disregard of the international community would help him achieve control of Yugoslavia. Yet he didn't set out to destroy the country, and was originally less nationalistic than Slovenia's Kučan and Croatia's Franjo Tudjman, whom he attempted to restrain. Realizing that he would obstruct their plans, the two leaders offered solutions they themselves weren't ready to accept, such as turning Yugoslavia into a confederation. They then complained that their republics' democratic aspirations were being thwarted by Milošević's communist hegemonism.

The West, in particular the U.S. and Germany, whose minister of foreign affairs, Hans-Dietrich Genscher, made himself available to Kučan around the clock, backed them up, and on 25 June 1991 Slovenia declared its independence. Its forces blockaded JNA barracks in its territory and seized control of the borders. Yugoslav soldiers were completely unprepared for an attack from within the federation and orders to counter the blockade and recapture borders were rescinded as soon as the first casualties were counted. Slovenia initiated the bloodshed, and in all fifty soldiers died in what amounted to an operetta war, but the western media reported that hordes of Serbian communists were razing Slovenia's cities.

Milošević and the general staff, by then primarily composed of Serbs and Montenegrins, planned to have the Slovenian leadership arrested but desisted when they realized a Serbian-backed coup in Slovenia would inevitably lead to civil war. The general staff wasn't prepared to assume responsibility for a coup, and Milošević realized that if they were so prepared, they might not hesitate to depose him as well.

Ultimately no one was more pleased by Slovenia's departure than Milošević. "Excellent," he said. "Now it'll be easier for the Croats to leave." And he was right. Franjo Tudjman was following Kučan's lead, and on 7 October 1991 Croatia's parliament announced that sovereignty, "a Croat dream for thirteen centuries," was finally at hand.

Slovenia and Croatia had entered into an alliance prior to Slovenia's secession, but Slovenia's leadership was wary of Franjo Tudjman and felt that Milošević might reconsider his position toward Slovenia if they were to endorse Tudjman's position on the self-rule of Serbian enclaves in Croatia. On 12 August Franc Bučar, the president of Slovenia's parliament, and Dimitrije Rupel, the Slovenian minister of foreign affairs, had met in Belgrade with Dobrica Ćosić, a Serb nationalist author and dissident during the Tito era. They offered to remain neutral in any conflict between Serbia and Croatia regarding the enclaves if Serbia would agree to an alliance with Slovenia. An agreement was drafted, and Ćosić briefed Milošević, who reluctantly promised to speak with Kučan but insisted that the Slovenes weren't to be trusted.

On 20 October 1991 the JNA pulled out of its barracks in Slovenia, and on 5 December former Yugoslavia's last president, Stipe Mesić, cheerfully announced that he was out of a job. The federation no longer existed, and the Croatian leadership expressed its appreciation in rounds of hearty applause.

But bitter civil wars soon erupted in Croatia and Bosnia. Despite a massive effort to mobilize the Serbian nation, and a steady stream of casualties, Milošević denied that Serbia was at war, and told U.S. Ambassador Warren Zimmerman that "not a single citizen of Serbia" was fighting in Bosnia or Croatia, and that he had never heard of Arkan's Tigers or any other paramilitary organization. Meanwhile, the Tigers were training recruits in Belgrade's largest sports arena, and according to Vojislav Šešelj, the leader of Serbia's Radical Party, Milošević had the JNA channel thirty thousand firearms to his own paramilitaries.

Yugoslavia had been established seventy years earlier to promote the well-being of kindred peoples, and while Milošević was hardly an innocent bystander, the Slovenes were ultimately responsible for the war. Yet they won their side of the conflict without having to engage in a real battle and profited from the ensuing misery by supplying arms to Alia Izetbegović's forces in Bosnia. Five years later when Slovenia became an associate of the European Union, Bill Clinton congratulated the republic and noted that it was being rewarded for not having participated in the wars. The Slovenes then became the first citizens of a former communist block country to be allowed to enter the U.S. without visas. Congratulations indeed!

In his first years in power, Miloševié did not travel beyond Yugo-slav borders and only left Serbia twice. On the few occasions he felt allies were needed, he looked for them in the wrong places. His attempts to win Israel's support were a complete failure. He hosted Russia's nationalist communists, believing they would emerge victorious against Gorbachev and Yeltsin, whom he opposed. He was constantly hatching laughable schemes such as a confederation between Serbia and Greece. It first became appar-ent that Serbia was becoming a pariah state in 1989 when western ambassadors refused to attend a commemoration of the battle of Kosovo Polje. Miloševié could not bear the affront. Far from being diplomatic, he retaliated against U.S. Ambassador Warren Zim-merman, the representative of the world's greatest power, by refusing to see him for eight months.

But internally Serbian and Montenegrin members of the Yugo-slav presidency obtained everything Miloševié wanted. Borislav Jović was the dean of Serbian officials. He began his career as director of the Zastava automotive plant in Kragujevac and joined the Yugoslav leadership in the early 1970s. He had also reported to Ivan Stambolić and became close to Miloševié, then his main rival. Extremely energetic, inscrutable, unflappable, and stubborn, he radiated such tension that he could drive people to nervous collapse. He was also arrogant and often led others to the conclu-sion that "nothing can be accomplished with the Serbs." It was impossible to negotiate with him, and he claimed with pride that people could either try to oppose him, or submit. He later boasted that while presiding over the Yugoslav Party he would often challenge his committee members to accomplish even one-tenth of what he could and wryly noted that he had a "bad habit of corner-ing them into all-night meetings."

Having risen to office on a wave of popular support in Montenegro, Dr Branko Kostić became president of the Yugoslav leadership when Croatia and Slovenia seceded. He was eloquent, like Jović, unflappable and inscrutable, and built like a brick wall. Called "Branko Bones" by his peers because of his love of gam-bling, he brought his criminal sensibilities into politics. He consistently voted against Croatia's Stipe Mesić during voting within the Presidency and is reported to have encouraged the war. His youngest brother volunteered for combat, and he himself frequently visited the troops. During the wars in Croatia and Slovenia he worked closely with the military leadership and seemed to enjoy it. He disciplined and decorated personnel and ordered a massive purge of the general staff. In wake of the conflict in Croatia and the JNA's humiliating retreat from its barracks in Slovenia, he awarded eighty citations for bravery to soldiers who had massacred civilians in Vukovar. "I am convinced," he said, "that you will continue to carry out your missions honourably and successfully, for the benefit of our people in these regions."

This Montenegrin, who claims that his clan was founded in 1650, was an intense proponent of Serbian and Montenegrin unity. When a reporter asked him what difference there was between Montenegrins and Serbs, Kostić replied that "the difference is that a vast majority of Montenegrins can say they are Serbs, while a vast majority of Serbs cannot say they are Montenegrins." Serbs and Montenegrins were generally impressed, and one group even petitioned that, given Kostić's military achievements, he be proclaimed a national hero. It was with leaders such as Kostić, Jović, and Milošević that Serbs and Montenegrins faced their future, convinced they were on the verge of great historical victories and the realization of the age-old dream of Serbian unity.

Though Serb nationalism was at its peak, most Serb citizens didn't wish to fight, and countless young men became deserters. They fled across borders, went into hiding, or simply refused to bear arms. Only 26 per cent of eligible Serbs presented themselves for conscription, many of them torn between their sense of duty and fear. In Bosnia a JNA commander had conscripts form two lines, one for soldiers and another for "chickens" who wanted to go home. A young man named Miroslav Milenković changed his mind a number of times, then stopped in the middle and shot himself in the head.

Heavy sanctions were imposed on Milošević's Yugoslavia, and the western media branded all Serbs as criminals, not even bothering to investigate when they were accused of atrocities. But Serb nationalists relished their notoriety and only made matters worse by destroying Vukovar and shelling Dubrovnik, two cultural and historic landmarks, mounting a three-year siege of Sarajevo, and threatening to bomb Vienna, Rome, Zagreb, and even London. On one memorable occasion a Serb commander, no doubt wishing to impress reporters from CNN, ordered his artillery to release a salvo on camera. "For CNN," he intoned, "fire on Goradže!" No one could have harmed Serbia more than its own frenzied nationalists.

The history of the war must still be written. Although the number of casualties remains unknown, all sides claimed as many as were convenient for their propaganda. Croats and Muslims concealed their crimes, but Serbs either gloried in their destructive might or claimed the jurisdiction of a higher court. Serbian author Brana Crnčević remarked, "Serbs don't kill out of hatred but out of despair. Killing out of despair is God's business, while killing out of hatred is the business of murderers and Satan. Serbian crimes are within God's jurisdiction, and the others are of the Devil's party."

In war, propaganda has historically been a powerful political weapon. There are, however, few examples of either malevolent or benign use of the media as striking as those that occurred during Yugoslavia's breakdown. Ljubljana was the first republic to unlock the media's potential, and Zagreb and Sarajevo followed. According to Gianni de Michelis, the entire Ljubljana brain-trust provoked the conflict in Slovenia in order to transfer their responsibility for Yugoslavia's collapse onto Belgrade. U.S. experts were hired to direct public opinion, and lies about the number of casualties, rapes, and persecutions attained monstrous levels. All sides inflated and diminished the real counts, and those in control of the media imposed their own version of the truth. For instance, the numbers of Muslim women raped were variously reported at 20,000, then 30,000, and even 150,000. Six years later a UN report concluded that 115 women from all three nationalities were raped during the conflicts.

Serbs, and only Serbs, were cast as a murderous horde overcome by madness and destructive hatred. The international media never questioned the accusations and grimly reported that Serbs were committing all the atrocities. Even *Newsweek* reported that Muslim women were being raped three times a day, tied with wire to a fence, drenched in gasoline, and burned alive. Under the influence of similar portrayals and televized fabrications, people in the West were completely horrified, and one journalist noted that even pacifists would have been happy to hear that an atomic bomb had been dropped on Belgrade.

Eight years after the fact, the Slovenes acknowledged that their freedom fighters had executed prisoners of war and fired on wounded soldiers. The Croats then acknowledged that they had shelled Šibenik, their own city, in order to compromise the Serbs. Yasushi Akashi, the UN under-secretary for humanitarian affairs, confirmed that Alia Izetbegović's Bosnian forces were similarly responsible for the shelling of Sarajevo's Markale marketplace in which sixty-eight civilians were killed.

Milošević was severely mistaken in disregarding diplomacy, but his misappraisal of international opinion had even graver consequences. While all sides lied during the war, Serbian propaganda was so inept that even the truths it told appeared as lies. In a communist mould, the leadership felt that all western media were pernicious and needed to be avoided at all costs. Their only concern was to keep the national press in line.

Propaganda is a powerful weapon, but the leadership's policies crippled our ability to use it to our advantage. Many talented, independently minded reporters were replaced by random quacks, clairvoyants, and obscure commentators – arrogant types who verbally assassinated opponents of the regime's belligerent policies, all under the auspices of "national security." It was a time when, by all standards, Serbia was ruled by the worst possible types and became destined for scorn and isolation.

During a round table organized by Ljubljana Television, Zdravko Tomac, a Croatian political scientist, blamed Milan Kučan: "Without Kućan, history would be different today." Stipe Mesić, who had become the leader of Croatia's parliament, agreed, adding that "Pope John Paul II, and Hans Dietrich Genscher, German minister of foreign affairs, were instrumental on the outside." Adem Demaci, a Kosovar Albanian leader, disagreed and insisted that the spark that led to Yugoslavia's collapse was in fact Kosovo. "Everything began in the late 1960s with the words 'Kosovo - Republic,'" he said. Mesić then boasted that he had been in constant touch with both Genscher and the Vatican while he was president of the Yugoslav Presidency and had provided the Pentagon with classified military information.

Milošević didn't need to boast, and though he denied responsibility for the collapse of former Yugoslavia, his actions proved

otherwise. He bullied the other republics, deceived and manipulated Serbs, and – ignoring the geopolitical consequences of the
Eastern Blok's collapse, especially German reunification – was
convinced the endgame would unravel in a contest of wills well
within Yugoslav borders and politics.

On 16 March 1991 during a secret meeting with Croatian and
Bosnian Serb leaders, he suggested that borders were always determined by force and that it was therefore imperative that Serbs
be forceful. "Serbs have a legitimate right to inhabit a single state,
and if we have to fight, so be it. I hope they won't be stupid
enough to fight us, because even if we are idle and unproductive,
we sure can fight."

When the JNA withdrew from Slovenia, Genscher demanded
that Europe recognize Slovenian and Croatian independence,
which only whetted Milošević's territorial appetites. From then on
Yugoslavia, which had been a peaceful and apparently stable
country, became a land of despair and atrocities where the powerful victimized the weak, hardened criminals became heroes, and
the innocent were forced to fight for their survival. Approximately
two million citizens whose families had inhabited their homes for
generations began miserably to wander the planet in search of
asylum. They were lucky to be alive and courageously started
over from scratch.

Meanwhile, the JNA had no clear understanding of its objectives
and strategy. Ever since World War II, it had been a privileged,
unassailable institution which was said to guarantee Yugoslavia's
stability. However, it wasn't prepared for a civil war and fell apart
in the wake of its defeat in Slovenia. There were early indications
that the general staff would carry out a putsch, but they weren't
even capable of that – they too were divided along ethnic lines.
Tito's generals, not an entirely skilful group of people to begin
with, had gradually been replaced by lunatics eager to seize any
opportunity to become national leaders.

Veljko Kadijević was the minister of the armed forces. He and
his staff trusted Milošević, in their minds a politician who would
remain faithful to communism and uphold Yugoslavia, two
pillars of their support. In 1990, when Milošević brought in a
multiparty system, the five-pointed communist star remained
their insignia, and they demonstrated their communist faith by

supporting Mirjana Marković's Union of Communists–Movement for Yugoslavia. But after the defeat in Slovenia, the officers who remained on the general staff became Milošević's pawns.

Kadijević was a staunch Yugoslav of mixed Croat and Serb heritage. He was the only remaining member of the general staff to have fought with the partisans, and politicians respected his military skills. They regarded him as both a soldier and an intellectual, and military personnel respected his diplomatic and political skills. However, he failed to live up to their expectations. He used his military clout to threaten politicians, and was responsible for the humiliating defeat in Slovenia. Convinced that the army could prevent a civil war, he sought to impose martial law but ultimately didn't have the courage to send in his troops.

Milošević and Kadijević became close during holidays on the Adriatic coast, and on Serbia's recommendation Kadijević was made a four-star general. He and Milošević shared the opinion that Serbia and the JNA could uphold communist Yugoslavia. Kadijević maintained that it was the JNA's mission to protect territories with Serbian inhabitants, and he militarized these areas with the intent of defending Yugoslavia's prospective borders. But after the JNA's humiliating defeat and subsequent disintegration, Kadijević was no longer useful. He left his position with honours in late 1991, when Branko Kostić decorated him with the Order of the Yugoslav Star. By then he was weakened by illness and retired to a privileged enclave on the outskirts of Belgrade, insulated from all military and political concerns.

High hopes were placed on Ante Marković, a Croat who was the last prime minister of Yugoslavia and is remembered as a politician who sought change but failed to define it. He was in fact highly capable and was certainly the most pleasant individual to ever become Yugoslavia's prime minister. His tenure was marked by an attempt to modernize economic policy and create order, and resulted in a strong dinar, consumer confidence, and free currency exchanges. A well-spoken, able economist, he was also the only Yugoslav politician who enjoyed the trust of western leaders, and knew when to seek compromise with the nationalists. Always seeking to encourage mutual understanding, he endorsed a fortified Serbian constitution and even sliced a commemorative cake on which "Long Live Serbia" was written.

Ante Marković was systematically exploited and lied to by the nationalist government and, having founded a pro-Yugoslav reform party, he became their great satan. The intellectuals and the press hounded him, and Milošević, Tudjman, and Kućan were actually united against him. Ljubljana ridiculed him, Belgrade denounced him as a Croatian spy, and Zagreb declared that he was a "megalomaniacal criminal and immoral beast" which Belgrade had "bribed with meatballs." In August 1990 Borislav Jović, writing under the pseudonym S.L., pamphleteered against him in three issues of *Politika*. The president of the Communist Party of Yugoslavia had publicly disavowed the Yugoslav prime minister. Such was the sad state of affairs in Yugoslavia at the onset of the 1990s.

A *coup d'état* might have prevented civil war if there had been close collaboration between Ante Marković and Veljko Kadijević and support from influential bodies in Ljubljana, Zagreb, Belgrade, and the international community. None of these conditions was met; Marković and Kadijević were on good terms for only a short while, and neither possessed the courage to assume the risks involved in a coup, given that nationalists with broad popular support already controlled Serbia, Croatia, and Bosnia.

Ill-conceived western policies towards Yugoslavia didn't provide any rational solutions either but only contributed to the chaotic state of affairs. Yugoslavia's collapse served the interests of many nations in the West, but Germany's involvement was particularly decisive. Opposing any premature recognition of Slovenia and Croatia, U.S. envoy Cyrus Vance remarked that Genscher was "out of control" and that his actions were "insane." Still, the German Ministry of Foreign Affairs had orders to notify Genscher "wherever he may be, and at any time" Ljubljana called, and the Germans used propaganda, cash, arms, and intrigue to encourage Slovenia's secession, their main argument being the aggressive nature of Milošević's policies.

Given these circumstances, it is difficult to believe that Yugoslavia could have remained intact, but a more forceful western approach could certainly have compelled the leadership to avoid bloodshed. Instead, they were allowed to hatch their hopelessly flawed plots and destroy the federation.

On a number of occasions Milošević and the general staff plotted a coup. But Milošević never acknowledged his influence on the general staff, nor would he accept any responsibility for the outbreak of war. "I'll repeat myself a hundred times: I'm for peace, Serbia isn't at war," he said. Meanwhile there were massive conscriptions, coffins poured in from battlefields in Bosnia and Croatia, and newspapers were filled with obituaries that bitterly cited Milošević, such as the following: "Deceased, 23 May 1992 near Mostar, when 'Serbia wasn't at war' and 'not a single Serbian soldier was stationed outside of Serbia.'"

Milošević refused to acknowledge his responsibility regarding the bloody outcome of the Yugoslav crisis and collapse of the federal republic. "All three nations are guilty, but primarily responsibility falls on certain members of the international community," he said. His wife shared similar opinions. She accused foreign powers, nationalists, and Yugoslav emigrants, but she also consistently condemned Yugoslavia's destruction, war, and nationalism, which to her was "a monster far more offensive than anti-communism." But she did not consider her husband to be a nationalist and wouldn't acknowledge that he was in any way responsible for the violent breakup. And while young men were dodging mobilization in droves, she said she couldn't say whether the government was engaging in mobilization, and didn't believe it was. Marković never challenged her husband's policies, even though they led Serbia into darkness and allowed Croatia and Slovenia to realize their "age-old" dreams of independence.

8

A Leader in Need

Milošević's popularity peaked in 1991, during the war's early stages. The government of Serbia and that of the rump state of Yugoslavia were firmly under his control, as was the JNA, and military victories and the greater Serbian myth elated the population, who were like children who had been given a new toy. The realization of the old dream of Serb unity within a single state seemed close at hand, and prodded by Milošević's iron will, Serbs would see to its realization.

However, sanctions, wartime casualties, and isolation took their toll, and Serbia's euphoria soon faded. In 1992 Milošević encountered unprecedented setbacks, finding himself ahead of all contenders in contemporary atrocity sweepstakes. The West wanted to bomb Belgrade, Doctors Without Borders circulated a poster comparing him to Hitler, and Belgrade University went on strike. Pacifists held demonstrations during which people got down on their knees to pray for his resignation, and citizens protested the Siege of Sarajevo by marching past his headquarters bearing a kilometre-long mourning band. Eventually armoured vehicles and a triple cordon of police in riot gear used automatic weapons to protect Milošević's residence against students whose approaching chants terrified neighbourhood residents.

In an attempt to escape communism, there was a sudden desire to revive the Karadjordjević dynasty, and Prince Alexander visited Serbia twice, in October 1991 and early 1992. The leadership was opposed to his arrival but endeavoured to maintain order and tolerated yet another round of national euphoria, which it fully expected would subside. Behind the scenes Serbia's officials treated the prince with petty malice. The royal family's luggage was delayed an entire day "because it got lost somewhere," police failed to provide security, and RTB repeatedly aired the prince's stammering forays into Serbian, leading his supporters to complain that the "Serbian king can't even speak his people's language." The visits were portrayed as an expensive royal excursion, putting an end to royalist fantasies. Prince Alexander returned to his business concerns, and Serbia went back to living with Milošević. No longer as revered as he had been, encountering ever more serious setbacks but craving power, he needed to somehow assuage Serbia's discontent.

Shock therapies are often successful, and Milošević, who is inclined to create diversions with astonishing moves suggesting that he has evolved, announced that Dobrica Ćosić and Milan Panić would assume the federal leadership: Ćosić, a respected Serbian author and anti-communist, as president, and Panić, a Serbian-American industrialist who had proven himself in the competitive U.S. marketplace, as prime minister. Serbs were for once happy with Milošević's choice of personnel.

Ćosić's abilities far exceeded the powers Milošević granted him. He had been instrumental in the awakening of Serb nationalism and endorsed Milošević when he embraced nationalism. Though he didn't like government, influence appealed to him, as did the prospect of becoming a leader of the Serbian nation. Serbs throughout former Yugoslavia trusted him, and though he wasn't religious, the church respected him because he was an author who considered that Serb Orthodoxy was the nation's spiritual wellspring. He had also worked closely with Radovan Karadžić during the formation of the Bosnian Serbs' nationalist party, raising funds and persuading Karadžić to take its helm.

Ćosić realized that aggressive nationalism could only have disastrous consequences, yet he had been indifferent to the 8th Plenary Session, which had appeared to him to be a power struggle between Titoist factions. Although he denounced Milošević's autocratic rule, he often spoke admiringly of his "intense struggle for the Serbian people's rights."

Ćosić and Milošević first met in early 1990 during a contrived encounter from which a memorable parting exchange indicated

that a friendship would follow. "I hope to see you again," said
Milošević, to which Ćosić ambiguously replied, "We're neighbours – all that separates us is a fence." Grinning, Milošević noted
that he hoped the fence in question wasn't too high. They subsequently met quite often, always in Milošević's presidential office
and avoiding Mirjana Marković, whom Ćosić never met.

More than a quarter-century after quitting Tito's Communist
Party, Ćosić re-entered politics through the front door. At seventy-
two, having undergone three difficult rounds of surgery, he
became the head of an unrecognized state. Yugoslavia's precarious footing within the international community troubled him, and
he accepted the presidency because friends, public opinion, and
his devotion to Serbia and Montenegro made it impossible for him
to refuse.

Members of a divided opposition debated Yugoslavia's future,
all vying to become government officials. Ćosić was the only Serb
whose reputation and abilities were equal to the task of holding
them at bay. He was a natural leader, one to whom no one could
object, and while alternatives to Milošević's regime were being
suggested, Ćosić remained impartial, stating that he could only be
of use to Serbia as an impartial intellectual, a stance that eventually led him into conflict with both the opposition and the government.

Milošević didn't trust Ćosić, but having accepted the numerous
demands Ćosić warily placed on his acceptance of office – including regular elections, creating a leadership council, non-partisan
government, less rigid foreign policies, Serbianizing the JNA,
national consensus on all important matters, and compromise
with the opposition – Milošević was confident he would toe the
line. And though Ćosić had openly criticized Milošević's autocratic rule, catastrophic policies, and disastrous tardiness in
democratizing Serbia, he was now saying that "policies which do
not represent the will of all Serbs are not democratic," adding that
"in this regard, the Serbian government's current policies and
those of its president are appropriate."

Significantly Ćosić, the man who had initiated the Serb question and helped to organize Serbs in Kosovo, Croatia, and Bosnia,
predicted a disastrous consequence of Serbia's quarrels with the
other republics – namely, that Serbia's fate was being determined

in Washington. A year before he assumed the presidency, Ćosić noted that the Serbs' lack of flexibility is their greatest flaw and remarked that "we must abandon our poetic tendency to seek the impossible, [and must] seriously consider our mistakes, and formulate realistic goals."

Milan Panić is an emigrant who not only had a dream of embarking on a great adventure but was able to realize that dream. Starting out in America with only twenty dollars to his name, he built a commercial empire. After Dušan Mitević introduced him to Milošević, they became close friends. Observing that Panić was also politically naive, Milošević agreed with Mitević's suggestion that he would make an excellent prime minister. Thus Panić the emigrant, a man who had left Yugoslavia as a poor cyclist from Belgrade's periphery, would be returning as prime minister. With adventure still in his heart, Panić took the bait.

The well-considered strategy immediately foundered, for Panić announced that he would seek to dismiss Milošević "as soon as possible." Milošević was horrified. Panić, who was supposed to be a figurehead, either had a mind of his own or had been pressured by the Americans. In any case his candidacy had been announced, and there was little Milošević could do but wait.

Accompanied by Mitević, Panić arrived in Belgrade on 8 July 1992 and rushed to meet with Milošević. They had barely shaken hands when Panić enquired when he would resign. As Panić cheerfully continued to pressure him, Milošević remained surprisingly calm. "Our friendship must be compatible with Yugoslav interests," Panić said, and Milošević agreed.

"And Yugoslavia's interest is that you voluntarily resign."

"Are you sure?"

"I know where the Americans stand, and the West. They can't stand the Serbian regime, and sanctions won't be lifted until you're gone."

"You do think sanctions will be lifted then?" Milošević asked.

"I'm convinced they'll be lifted. I was promised they would be lifted. If something's to be done, you must leave, Slobodan."

"And what happens if I don't?"

"I leave and the agreement falls through. I withdraw without making a fuss."

At one point Panić became threatening. "Watch," he said, "I will count down from five [and I want your decision]. I'm counting: five, four, three, two ..." He wouldn't let it go, and as it was getting late, Milošević capitulated. "Everything we agree to will be confirmed by the White House," Panić insisted as Milošević ushered him out.

According to Dušan Mitević, Milošević seemed amenable to Panić's proposal and agreed that an agreement be drafted between the parties. Exiting his office, Mitević tried to persuade him that it was a good idea. "You'll be a popular hero again, because you'll be resigning to put an end to sanctions."

"That's fantastic," replied Milošević.

That evening Mitević, Panić, and Panić's advisor, John Scanlon, a former U.S. ambassador to Yugoslavia, drafted an agreement according to which the U.S. would lift sanctions against Yugoslavia as soon as Milošević resigned. Milošević and his family were also guaranteed freedom of movement, and he would become president of the Yugoslav–American Bank. But the following day Milošević told Mitević to forget the whole thing. Apparently he had felt defeated and truly considered resigning, but Mirjana Marković believed that he was still more effective than his opponents – "stronger" – and insisted that he stay put.

Ćosić also sought Milošević's resignation, though not as forcefully as Panić, and whenever the opposition asked that he force the issue, he replied that pressure would only cause trouble. While Milošević's Yugoslavia continued to be very much at odds with the international community, Ćosić and Panić were acceptable in the West, which put a lot of faith in them. Diplomatic avenues were once again open, and on the whole, Yugoslavs felt that their country was headed in the right direction.

Panić radiated self-confidence and was an extremely dedicated prime minister. He once visited sixteen countries in a span of thirty-five days, meeting with fifty leading politicians, including nine heads of state and ten ministers of foreign affairs, and courageously visited Sarajevo during the siege. But he also overestimated his authority, and his endless quips tended to offend people. For instance, he once said that Serbian politics were Mickey Mouse politics and that Serbian politicians should "go to Disneyland." He also commandeered Tito's Mercedes limousine, and as the armed forces were technically under his supervision, he didn't miss a single opportunity to engage the general staff. Witty, vain, and impulsive, he swaggered and was always grinning, whether or not he had a reason to do so, and was never caught at a disadvantage. When Lord Carrington, the former British foreign secretary, referred to him as "bogus president," he cheerfully countered with "bogus lord." He also told reporters that the Yugoslav constitution granted him powers similar to those Bush had under the U.S. constitution, and maintained that Milošević's powers were similar to those of U.S. governors.

"Let Milošević go about his business, and may God help him! I'll fight anyone who stands in my way," Panić promised. From the onset of his term in office, he was fair game for all the hatred, humiliation, and scorn Milošević's people could muster. But as he remained oblivious to their attacks, all they could do was laugh at him, and eventually as a gesture of appreciation, the general staff even presented him with four parade uniforms.

Relations between Milošević, Ćosić, and Panić worsened in late August during a two-day conference in London that Milošević recalls as one of his most unpleasant experiences. Panić and the western delegates called for his immediate resignation and otherwise ignored him. According to one participant, Milošević felt like a beaten dog, and it appeared that he would return to Belgrade an ordinary citizen. But the Serbian president was to be feared most when he felt threatened. He refused to resign and decided that upon his return to Belgrade he would oust Panić.

His first two attempts were unsuccessful. On the first occasion Milošević had to relent when students threatened massive protests. On the second, Ćosić, the opposition, and the Montenegrins intervened, and Yugoslavia's parliament voted to keep Panić in office. Panić's prime ministership was temporarily secure, but the conflict between him and Milošević only grew more intense.

The two opponents' final meeting was held 8 October 1992. At the last minute Dušan Mitević was asked to join to witness their agreement regarding Milošević's resignation. Panić insisted that Milošević had reneged and showed him the draft of their agreement.

Milošević replied that they had only discussed the matter, and turned to Mitević. "Duško, did you sign anything?"

"No, I didn't."

"Did I sign anything?"

"No, you didn't."

"So that's just a piece of paper," Milošević concluded. Over lunch, which included more wine than Panić was accustomed to, the conversation deteriorated. Panić said he would show up with his generals and have Milošević arrested, to which Milošević replied that Panić had better stay at home.

"Why should I stay at home?"

"Because," Milošević replied, "I'll arrest and probably execute the generals."

Panić then accused Milošević of being the "new Hitler." Yet at other points their meeting was cordial, and they behaved as though they were old friends. Panić and Mitević left Milošević's office at around 7:30 P.M. Panić was tired. He asked Mitević what he thought Milošević wanted out of their meeting.

"He declared war on you," Mitević replied.

"Then war it is!" said Panić.

Milošević knew his adversaries better than they knew him. Neither Ćosić nor Panić were risk-takers, nor would they avail themselves of deceit or force. Milošević opted for all-out war, which he declared the following day during a television interview. His confidence and defiance were apparent, as was his determination. He wouldn't bend for anyone, least of all the Americans before whom everyone else crawled.

Milošević controlled the Serbian police and Yugoslav armed forces. But in addition to a few concerns he had regarding the loyalty of a few socialists, he warily kept an eye on the highly organized and well-equipped federal police through his agents on the force and through politicians involved in state security. The federal police remained loyal to the federal leadership, as had been demonstrated when Panić had Mihalj Kertes dismissed from its ranks when he correctly assumed that Kertes, who had mysteriously appeared in London, was spying on him. Still, the Serbian police and 70,000 members of the armed forces were loyal to Milošević, and on Saturday, 19 October 1992, when all was quiet in Belgrade, members of the Serbian police penetrated and seized their federal counterparts' headquarters. Citizens were told that the building belonged to Serbia and had merely been repossessed, but everyone knew that it contained documents on informants, individuals involved in Yugoslavia's collapse, and paramilitary organizations that could compromise the regime. More importantly, Panić and Ćosić were no longer served by a security apparatus.

The seizure was the most stunning criminal act in the history of Yugoslavia's security forces, and both abroad and in Yugoslavia there were rumours of a coup. Ćosić was in Geneva at the time with Tudjman and unsuccessfully tried to contact Milošević. When Tudjman asked what was going on in Belgrade, Ćosić merely told him that the Serbian police were causing some trouble.

Milošević had committed an extremely serious offence that reflected both his political irresponsibility and felonious nature. It was an opportunity for Ćosić to act boldly and have Milošević impeached, but bold leadership wasn't among Ćosić's attributes. He later explained that the measure of support he would have received from the JNA, the opposition, and the Montenegrins was generally overestimated but acknowledged that he should have resigned in protest. That would have provoked a political crisis from which "Milošević and his party mob" wouldn't have easily recovered. Milošević easily rejected his request that Yugoslavia's parliament rise in defence of the constitution, Ćosić said:

I repeated my request, but it fell on deaf ears because Milošević ... had ordered them to reject my motions. I called a meeting of the Federal Policy Council, and Milan Panić and I tried to bring the usurper to his senses. But [his allies] brazenly lied and misrepresented the facts, and as Yugoslavia was truncated, I did not know where to turn. Elections had been scheduled, and we were slowly re-establishing relations with the West. We had pledged our cooperation in London, but the war in Bosnia was still raging. Could I resign and lead the country into yet greater chaos and uncertainty? Panić's resignation would certainly have followed, and these questions plagued me for days on end. Upon advice from my friends, I concluded that it was more rational to remain and work the international front, a decision I was most notably supported in by Douglas Hurd, the British foreign secretary. I hoped the elections would alter the balance of power in parliament, and believed that Slobodan Milošević would realize that his despotic obstinacy was harmful. However, [he] won because Serbs did not have the sense to vote otherwise, and I did not have the courage to tender my resignation and set the country on a sure path to ruin.

An opportunity to unseat Milošević had slipped by, but a more conventional and promising one would present itself in December 1992 during Serbia's presidential election. Ćosić's candidacy would have been a threat to Milošević; he was a respected author whose support flowed from the nation's grass roots, and there were doubts that Milošević would even face him. Many people, including Cyrus Vance and David Owen, co-chairmen of the conference on former Yugoslavia, tried to persuade him to enter the race, but to the great dismay of his allies he refused, and his refusal eventually led to his banishment from politics.

Milošević could breathe more easily, but his troubles were far from over. Panić wasn't to be easily dismissed and inaugurated his American-style campaign on 1 December 1992, with tremendous support from students, who had collected thirty thousand signatures endorsing his candidacy. He then embarked on a whirlwind tour of the country during which he made emotional appeals to end the war and visited countless citizens, including peasants, in their homes.

Meanwhile Milošević was being greeted by sustained catcalls but made sure they were edited from RTB's soundtracks. Serbs were still buoyed by their military victories in Bosnia and Croatia, and as the national reserves weren't yet depleted, the full effects of sanctions hadn't been felt. "Serbia will not relent or sway but look everyone in the eye," Milošević maintained, opposing Panić's plan to implement a policy of democratic compromise in which "Serbs and their nation's dignity" wouldn't suffer. Propaganda declared that Serbia was invincible, and the airwaves, press, and streets were filled with slogans like "We're on the right track!" and "Unrelenting Serbia!" According to Milošević, it was evident that we wouldn't "go hungry or freeze" as a result of sanctions, nor would we be "seized by fear."

Ćosić condemned Milošević's refusal to compromise with the West, stating that he differed in his "understanding of democracy, the nature of the new state, and various means and ends of foreign policy, with particular regard to the evaluation of the effects of sanctions." But though his sympathies went to Panić, he generally kept his distance due to "unexpected differences" between them, most notably Panić's "method of developing government policies." Though Ćosić refused to enter the race, he endorsed parties that adopted his agenda. It was a strategy Milošević would later exploit, and it eventually led to the opposition blaming Ćosić for its defeat. Ćosić has suggested he stayed out of the race because he had no political party of his own and couldn't therefore have brought about any change had he won. He didn't offer more support to Panić, he said, because as Yugoslavia's president he was bound to non-partisan behaviour.

Milošević won the election with 2,515,047 votes against Panić's 1,516,693. Panić did extremely well, considering that the campaign had only lasted seven days, the Albanians boycotted the election, the opposition was divided, and – last but not least – the media and polls were controlled by Milošević.

Suddenly Tito's limousine was no longer at Panić's disposal, and in December 1992 he was harrassed and almost arrested by police. Ćosić intervened with Milošević, who told him, "We'll arrest him and shave his head, and then you fire him." It's hard to say whether he was seriously considering Panić's arrest or merely wanted to flex his muscles, and in the end he cheerfully relented and told Ćosić that he could have Panić, as though he were doing him a personal favour.

Panić's brief and amateurish political career had come to an end. He had courageously entered the fray, and now he accepted defeat, remaining convinced that he would soon be vindicated. But nothing really changed upon his departure, except that Milošević's hold on the federal government became more substantial, which helped Montenegro and Serbia drift apart.

But Ćosić learned nothing from these events, and his conflict with the Serbian government and opposition grew more intense. He denounced the government's obstruction of the federal leadership and manipulation of public opinion and accused the opposition of supporting paramilitary organizations in Bosnia that oppressed, looted, and terrorized local populations. He was subsequently blackballed, but he knew the Serbs wouldn't be able to achieve their territorial objectives in Croatia. He tried to salvage what he could by appealing to Franjo Tudjman, with whom he agreed that borders between Serbia and Croatia would remain intact if Tudjman would seek a solution to the problems facing Serbs in Croatia. When Milošević heard about the agreement, he had the Croatian Serb leadership issue a statement disputing Ćosić's right to represent Croatia's Serbs and declared that the agreement was a "treasonous, anti-Orthodox conspiracy."

It was obvious that Milošević wouldn't spare Ćosić, even though Ćosić had spared him. The only question was how he was going to bring about Ćosić's demise. But he was in no rush and the two worked closely after Panić's departure. Both supported the Vance-Owen plan, and the West's pragmatic leaders respected Milošević's electoral victory. But as soon as Milošević felt assured that his presidency and international status were secure, he moved against Ćosić.

Ćosić gave the impression of being a clever man, but he often spoke carelessly, even during his presidency. On 27 May 1993 he was invited to a routine meeting of the general staff. When he enquired about the agenda, General Života Panić, the chief of staff, replied they would be discussing the JNA's financial and personnel problems. Towards the end of the meeting, Ćosić invited his hosts to "freely criticize" him and his policies, adding that Yugoslavia was in a terrible predicament and that many people were asking him why he didn't "take action." It was a casual remark, meant to highlight the magnitude of Yugoslavia's crisis, and Ćosić's last words to General Panić were to the effect that politicians should never resort to violent means. But no stenographer was present, the meeting wasn't taped, and notes taken by a pair of colonels were used as evidence that Ćosić had attempted to "violate the constitution."

Though it remains unclear whether General Panić or one of his colleagues decided to misrepresent Ćosić's remarks, their move was perhaps related to Ćosić's call for an enquiry into commercial dealings between the JNA and the general's son. In any case Milošević knew that Ćosić wouldn't have involved himself in a coup, but as he was the last obstacle to his authority over the federal government, he had to be removed. Thus Milošević, who had usurped the federal government's powers, accused Ćosić, who was in fact powerless, of violating the constitution. On 31 May 1992, three days after Ćosić's meeting with the general staff, Milošević had him impeached. There is no doubt that Ćosić was

Serbia's best alternative to Milošević, and that he and Milan Panić had done their best to set the nation on a conciliatory path. Thanks to them, Milošević was able to weather the international storm and susbsequently took credit for their efforts to end the wars in Bosnia and Croatia.

Opinions were divided regarding Čosić's term in office. By and large the Serbian people still respected him, but his enemies in the opposition felt he deserved to be punished for collaborating with Milošević. His presidency was noted for its refreshing style and his democratic rapport with the country's institutions, but he had no party of his own, the opposition was too divided to unite against the regime, the Montenegrins chose to remain neutral, and though the general staff initially favoured him, their support was never substantial.

Furthermore, Čosić wasn't prepared to avail himself of the same indiscriminate means that Milošević used. Čosić and Milan Panić had enabled him to survive the West's condemnation and were then ousted in the name of the nation's right to sovereignty. Milošević was now Yugoslavia's undisputed leader, and the nation continued to self-destruct.

Though Milošević had held on to power with astonishing ease, he no longer took risks with potential opponents in the federal leadership and replaced Čosić and Panić with Zoran Lilić and Radoje Kontić, both faceless and entirely loyal bureaucrats. Lilić's mother-in-law was terrified to hear that he had been entrusted with the presidency, but he became the perfect figurehead Milošević expected him to be, enjoying the office's privileges and never complaining that he wasn't consulted on matters of state.

9

The Oracle of Belgrade

Mirjana Marković was involved in all of her husband's decisions, but only stepped into the limelight in late 1988, during the so-called bureaucratic revolution. Gone were the days of her anonymity. Throughout the 1990s she was a key part of the political life of Serbia. Not satisfied with being simply a powerful woman, she wanted to be at the very top. She achieved this desire by eventually forming her own party, which would effectively rule Serbia.

In July 1994 Marković had consolidated twenty-three Marxist parties to create the Yugoslav United Left (YUL). In what she considered poetic symmetry, YUL, written in Serbian as JUL, is also the name of a summer month, and the founding congress was held then – the month of Mira's birth. The first congress was a spectacular event, combining the music of Brahms and Tchaikovsky with that of traditional Second World War partisan marching songs. Mirjana Marković was the focus of attention.

Milošević unofficially endorsed the new party by appearing at the reception that followed the congress as well as subsequent YUL functions. YUL with Mirjana Marković quickly became the new centre of power. She did not need popular votes to have a strong, influential party. Her wedding ring was enough.

Her pro-Yugoslav Marxist sensibilities were offended by the nationalist rallies. But since they broadened her husband's political base, she found a justification for them, saying that they were evidence of renewed participation in the political process by the masses and represented a virtuous struggle for the affirmation of Serbian interests in Yugoslavia. In her mind these rallies showed no animosity towards other Yugoslav nationalities. And when it was suggested that her husband had become the father of the Serbian nation, she replied, "Our citizens ... only need a president with a limited mandate."

When the party was inaugurated, Marković announced that its primary objective was to promote the welfare of disadvantaged citizens. However, it soon became apparent that none of these were among its membership. When Marković was asked to clarify the situation, she replied that Yugoslavia's poor were being deceived by the nationalists and would join her party as they understood that national, cultural, political, and economic interests cannot be separated.

YUL cunningly combined financial and political power. Early on it inherited the premises of the Communist Party–Movement for Yugoslavia (CP-MY). The CP-MY was closely connected with the army; the army – JNA – had given to CP-MY, and subsequently to YUL, U.S.$5 million from their own funds to finance their political activity. Thus money from the budget poured directly into YUL. Cronyism, favouritism, and slush funds were an important part of Marković's mechanism of influence. Membership in YUL became the best and quickest way to wealth and prestige and an essential prerequisite for all major business transactions, controlled through her personal monopoly of political power. Instead of addressing the needy, the traditional activity of the left, Marković became known as the patron saint of profiteers, sycophants, and wretched cowards.

YUL was able to supercede the Socialist Party because it functioned as a clearing house for government concessions, and its ranks swelled with corrupt officials and state company executives, mobsters, and sundry "entrepreneurs." The party projected an image of glamour by recruiting members of the cultural establishment and entertainment industry, in particular highly popular folk singers. Shortly after YUL was inaugurated, for instance, Marković, who usually avoided official roles in politics (none of which could possibly compete with the power her marriage conferred upon her), stepped down from the presidency of YUL in favour of Ljubiša Ristić. He was a prominent and avant-garde director in the theatre whose closest friends later said that they would have been less surprised to hear that he had become an astronaut.

Proud of her doctorate in sociology, Marković spared no effort to convince the public that she was also an outstanding intellectual. Throughout the 1990s she wrote a diary published in *Duga*, a Belgrade weekly, and in *Bazar*, a women's magazine. It was a strikingly odd mixture of propaganda, moralizing pedagogy, and trite lyricism in which she went on and on about the blessings of socialism, bird song, and the smell of freshly mown grass but never once mentioned the harsh realities of Serbian life. She also endorsed and excoriated politicians in her columns, just as their political fortunes were about to rise or fall. Since Milošević ruled behind closed doors and rarely commented publicly on anything he was doing, his wife's columns became known in Belgrade as the "Political Horoscope" and were closely watched, praised by the official press and ridiculed and sneered at by others. Dobrica Ćosić, Milan Panić, Radovan Karadžić, and Montenegro's Milo Djukanović, who all came into conflict with Milošević, significantly were all initially targeted in Marković's diary. She became the most reliable of oracles. Officials and party politicians were well advised to pay attention.

In 1994 the diaries were published in book form and praised as a first-class literary and philosophical achievement. While the works of talented Serbian authors went unpublished, donors eager to receive government contracts ensured that Marković's book was translated into about twenty different languages. A particularly well-informed Belgrade reviewer then noted that the collection had become Bill Clinton's favourite book. Fortunately others were more courageous and wrote that it was in fact a mixture of "kitsch, neuroses, and the hallucinations of a narcissistic woman." Slobodan Milošević was very proud of the "talents" and accomplishments of his wife. Together with their daughter, Marija, and son, Marko, he was an enthusiastic reader of her columns. Possessing a relatively limited education and even more limited interests, he believed the official press's claim that his wife's writings were second to none.

Marković's aspirations increased in proportion to the powers she gradually but unequivocally took over from her husband. She became the power that counts, hiring and firing officials, controlling the media, and generally setting the domestic agenda. She also became an ambassador at large. While Milošević hated travelling, she crossed the globe from London to Beijing. Officially she travelled broadly to promote her books. Unofficially she was treated everywhere as Milošević's wife and a person at the centre of power. Milošević, showing signs of fatigue, gladly ceded the controls to Mirjana, whom he loved and trusted. Eventually she indicated that "if a woman, despite completely ordinary talents, is capable of undoing even the best of men ... she deserves to enter the next century as his master." Marković's followers could only agree, and ensured that alongside their master, Serbia had also now a mistress to obey.

10

Serb against Serb

Milošević's hold on power was threatened by continued unrest in Yugoslavia, but he stayed afloat by distributing what remained of the national reserves. However, the international community was losing patience with futile diplomatic attempts to put an end to the war in Bosnia, and during the spring of 1993, when the West's sanctions and military actions intensified, Milošević turned against the Bosnian Serbs. In Serbia people either felt betrayed or welcomed the turnaround as the only rational solution to the conflicts.

The Bosnian Serbs had celebrated Milošević, but there were profound differences between them. While they were for the most part Serb Orthodox monarchists, Milošević's regime was still essentially communist. But regardless of their ideological differences, they accepted Milošević's leadership until the international community pressured him to oppose their warmongering.

Radovan Karadžić, the leader of the Bosnian Serbs, had spent most of his life in Sarajevo, where he was a psychiatrist. Hardly at peace with his own demons, he once spent a year in Belgrade hoping to find himself. But a U.S. sojourn was more profitable, in that he qualified there as a specialist in the treatment of depression, and also learned English. He had published four volumes of poetry, and his favourite instrument was the *gusla*, a one-stringed lute on which he entertained former U.S. president Jimmy Carter on the eve of a conference in Bosnia.

Karadžić looked more like a discus-thrower than a psychiatrist and entered politics late in life, during the Serb awakening when no one remained indifferent to politics. His interests were broad, and he was an eloquent, personable, and reassuringly patient individual who became a beloved, highly respected leader among Serbs. But behind a veneer of faultless composure was a defiant gambler who fanatically believed that only force and intransigence would pay off, and who justified his murderous quest for territory and independence with folksy rhetoric. "While Bosnia's Serbs don't need to eat, they can't live without their own country," he once said, adding that he had seen "amputees with joyous expressions on their faces" because they knew he wouldn't let them down. And when a Japanese reporter pointed out that the Siege of Sarajevo demonstrated that the Bosnian Serbs were in fact a bane, Karadžić replied, "Vipers are caught by the head."

Though Karadžić was intractable and didn't care about the suffering he caused, he was the most conciliatory member of the Bosnian Serb leadership. Less so was General Ratko Mladić, who also enjoyed broad popular support. Mladić was born in a Bosnian village two years before his father's heroic death at the end of World War II; as an impoverished fifteen-year-old orphan of war, he was admitted into military school, where he distinguished himself through talent and hard work. Later, having impressed the political leadership with his enterprising sense of command during the conflicts in Croatia, he became the Serb commander for all of Bosnia.

He was a typical soldier: disciplined, courageous, stubborn, and intensely goal-oriented. However, the notoriety he acquired during the war encouraged his tendency to make rash statements. He was soon threatening to bomb European capitals and, according to General Michael Rose, commander of the UN Protection Force in Bosnia, U.S. intelligence once intercepted Mladić's orders to pound Goradže so that "not even a toilet" remained intact. Mladić's western counterparts granted that he was an able military commander and even a "tactical genius," but they also said he was a "sadistic and extremely dangerous" man, accusations Mladić countered with statements like "People respect bullets." Mladić also told Muslims that his promises were as good as the Almighty's and warned them to be content with the territory he chose to leave them with, or else face his wrath. "In any case," he added, "it's more than enough for the likes of them." Even Karadžić said he needed to be gagged.

In an attempt to divide the Bosnian leadership, Milošević be-came close to Mladić. Having persuaded Karadžić to sign the Vance-Owen Plan that would have divided Bosnia into ten largely autonomous provinces, he seemed to be working to that end with Mladić as well. But Mladić intended to see the war through, and upon his intervention on 6 May 1993, the parliament of the Bos-nian Serbs' Republic of Srpska refused to ratify the agreement. Karadžić revoked Mladić's command, but the rank and file com-plained. Ćosić intervened, quoting one of George Washington's letters to Lafayette ("General, if we are not united today, we will hang together tomorrow"), and Mladić was quickly reinstated. Having understood that Mladić wasn't a reliable intermediary between himself and Karadžić, Milošević wrote him off and remarked, according to Richard Holbrooke, that he was "clinically insane."

Milošević's greatest personal defeats, and victories, occurred during his struggles with the Bosnian leadership. When the Vance-Owen Plan was rejected, he was humiliated and ridiculed in Belgrade. But once again Mirjana Marković's input was deci-sive. Though Milošević dealt with the Bosnian Serbs, they were anathema to her as anti-communists who refused to obey her husband. She declared war on Karadžić, calling his accusations of genocide against Bosnian Serbs an "utter, nonsensical lie." She reacted in like fashion to remarks made by Dr Biljana Plavšić, the Bosnian Serbs' vice-president, to the effect that Serbs would no longer tolerate the presence of Croats in their territories. Marković called Plavšić's views "psychopathic," reminiscent of those of another doctor: Mengele. Shortly thereafter Milošević began to speak in similar terms, though without referring to Plavšić. But after Plavšić refused to shake hands with him while he was trying to get the Bosnian Serbs to accept the Vance-Owen Plan, he decided it was time to take action.

Although he had made use of his considerable skills to tame the Bosnian leadership, his efforts proved futile. Karadžić and his associates realized that their territorial gains, which amounted to 70 per cent of Bosnia, meant they didn't have to accept the Vance-Owen Plan. The tide of war was in their favour, and they weren't prepared to relinquish what they had won in battle.

The international community continued to apply pressure on Milošević's regime, and on 4 August 1994 the Yugoslav government banned all members of the Bosnian Serb leadership from its territories. It blockaded the Drina River, the natural border between Serbia and Bosnia, and severed communications between the two republics. In a departure from his usual methods Miloševic then personally denounced the Bosnian Serbs, and the media followed suit. Suddenly they were no longer heroes but the "scourge of their own people." Serbs had often said that they were at odds with "the entire planet," and now they were divided among themselves. Their leaderships were divided, the opposition was divided, the populations of Serbia proper and Serbs across the Drina were divided. Everyone had an opinion, an excuse, and privileged access to the truth. Was Milošević entitled to act the way he did? Did the Bosnian leadership, which had benefited from Serbian assistance and spoke endearingly of "Mother Serbia," have any right to imperil her by defying the international community? And what sort of future lay in store for Serbs when they failed to get along at such crucial moments?

No one had expected such a radical turnabout from Milošević, least of all his victims, who had been convinced that he wouldn't dare treat his Serb brethren the way he was treated by the West, suffocating them and assuming responsibility before history for the eventual failure of the nation's struggle in Bosnia. But Miloševic's mind worked differently. His authoritarian wrath had been provoked by their refusal to comply with his wishes, and he was convinced that they would soon yield.

The church had become politicized upon the collapse of the former communist regime and played an active role in the Serb national awakening in Bosnia. But though it had unilaterally condemned the war and all atrocities and persecutions, it felt that Karadžić's struggle for national freedom was just. The views of a few hawkish bishops even caused some confusion among the flock. A highly anticipated bishophric council was finally held on the matter on 10 August 1994. Assuming tremendous responsibility for the nation's future, the church declared its continued support of Karadžić. "Just peace is the only lasting peace, while unjust peace is the source of all further suffering, and renewed conflict," it resolved.

Serbs were exhausted by war, humiliation, and poverty and would gladly have welcomed peace. But unfortunately, whenever Milošević agreed to policies the people sought, he implemented them in ways that made everyone feel cheated. He had said that the West's sanctions against Yugoslavia were "genocidal," but those he inflicted on his own people across the Drina were even more drastic. Having himself incited Serb nationalism in Bosnia and assisted the Bosnian Serb leadership during the war, he was now acting as though they were the only culprits.

The Bosnian Serbs' reaction was unexpected. Not only was the belligerence of these "stubborn" and misunderstood Bosnians no longer apparent but they even accepted the blockade and demonstrated remorse. Karadžić said there was nothing personal in Milošević's action. He added, "A mother is entitled to slap her child, but a child has no right to raise its hand against its mother."

There were dramatic differences of opinion. Milošević was alternately seen as a vile traitor, ready to lop off Karadžić's head and send it to Washington, or he was an insightful statesman seeking a rational exit to the great tragedy that had befallen our nation. He did, however, achieve his most important objective: the West's pragmatic leaders no longer sought his departure but embraced him as a trustworthy counterpart who could put an end to the war in Bosnia. The former "Butcher of the Balkans" was now a "mature politician" who clearly sought peace, and the "only Serb leader" who looked beyond the immediate future. Milošević's autocratic rule was suddenly appropriate, and for the time being all was forgiven.

History had repeated itself. Serbs, who had been at odds regarding the war, were now arguing over the terms of peace, including the future of Yugoslavia and that of their compatriots across the Drina, with whom they didn't even share a national anthem. During celebrations of St Vilnus Day in Kosovo members of the federal leadership arose during the Yugoslav anthem, while locals remained seated, and when a church choir sang an Orthodox hymn, the locals arose while members of the leadership remained seated. Lord Owen noted in his memoirs that the rift between Serbs was something that needed to be overcome but added that no one is better at dividing the Serbs than they are themselves.

11

Ruined Lives

Upon victory came defeat. During the mid-1990s it often seemed
that Serbia wouldn't survive, and the fact that Serbs weren't prepared for their ordeal only made matters worse. Citizens were
depressed and apathetic and hoped just to get through another
day. Milošević had started a war he wasn't able to end and had to
accept terms set by the world's great powers, primarily the U.S.
and Germany. The leadership had withdrawn its support to the
Bosnian Serbs, sapping both their military capacity and morale.
Abandoned by their motherland, they became impoverished and
literally went hungry and barefooted. Meanwhile the international
community sent aid to the Croats and Muslims, whose advantages steadily increased.

On 1 May 1995 the Miloševićs were in Karadjordjevo, enjoying
what had been one of Tito's favourite residences. Though no major celebrations were taking place, Serbs were still given the day
off as a token of their communist past. At dawn, while Serbia
slept, exhausted more by shortages and discontent than by hard
work, the Croatian Army rolled into the Croatian Serbs' Republic
of Krajina. They encountered no military opposition. Empty vil-
lages from which panic-stricken residents had fled were quickly
secured, and there was no word from Krajina's fearsome leaders,
who were perhaps also tired – of quarrelling over the presidency.
In a few short years, Milan Babić had replaced Jovan Rašković,
Goran Hadžić brought down Milan Babić, Milan Martić outwitted
Goran Hadžić, and Bora Mikelić undermined Martić – all under
the watchful eye of Slobodan Milošević, master of ceremonies.

Croatian soldiers entered the territory at dawn, and by 10:45 that night, Jasenovac, at the far end of the territory, had been captured. Meanwhile Serbia was enjoying a quiet holiday, as though the drama were unfolding in some desolate area across the globe. Television programming wasn't interrupted, and in Belgrade's entertainment district, people relaxed. There was no word from Milošević or any of his associates, nor was there any "greater Serbian" outrage. When Patriarch Pavle, head of the Serbian Orthodox Church, asked Milošević if Serbia would rise in defence of its brethren, Milošević only replied that everything was going "according to plan."

For the Krajinian population the invasion was a catastrophic nightmare. Fleeing misery and death, many sought haven in Serbia, where no one really cared about their problems. The republic was on the verge of explosive unrest, and government was wary of the additional problems their presence would bring. With the arrival of each successive column of refugees, the situation in Serbia grew more tense. The regime's propagandists suggested they go back and fight for their country, and Arkan (Zelko Raznjatovic), now a prominent Belgrade entrepreneur (even though he was wanted by Interpol and had spent his entire youth sowing death), said that as "a proud Serb" he would rather they "all died as heroes and were remembered as such."

While international envoys poured into Belgrade to meet with Milošević, Serbia's "leading proponent of peace," Serbian police embarked on a brutal mission to round up "deserters" – meaning all male refugees old enough to fight. Tens of thousands were tracked down like criminals in homes and in dormitories, in cafés and in the streets, and taken to the front. Heavily armed police captured thirty young men in a nightclub one night, including a few waiters who hadn't yet changed into their work clothes; sixty others, some wearing shorts, others in their pajamas, and a few in handcuffs, were hauled off to Pale, the Bosnian Serbs' capital.

Though Serbs in Serbia didn't wish to fight, they had been delighted by the victories of their brethren across the Drina. However, when the Bosnian Serbs' struggle became a lost cause, Serbia, which had encouraged their nationalist struggle, abandoned them. While Franjo Tudjman frequently visited the Croatian part of Bosnia, Milošević never went to Krajina himself. In their enthusiasm Serbs throughout former Yugoslavia had believed in his leadership and felt it was an honour to be on his side. But now it was all over. A monumental mistake had been made, and Serbia was at an all-time low.

On 5 August 1995 the Croatian Army captured Knin, the Krajinian capital, a Serbian stronghold in Croatia for over five hundred years. Once again there was no military resistance. Knin was eerily deserted but intact. Doors to many homes were left ajar, and hearths and television sets were still glowing, indicating that residents had fled in no more than a heartbeat. At noon the Croat commander, General Ivan Korada, unfurled the chequered Croatian flag over Knin's fortress. It was twenty metres long.

No single military campaign had ever resulted in such effortlessly significant gains, and regardless of the whereabouts of the defenders of the "indomitable Knin," residents fled for their lives. Apparently orders were given to withdraw temporarily, and the city's JNA defenders had no idea they wouldn't be returning. According to Bishop Amfilohije, the city had appeared entirely at peace just five days earlier when he visited President Martić and the two of them had a perfectly ordinary conversation.

Belgrade blamed Martić, and he in turn blamed Milošević and his "lackeys," Boris Mikelić and a group of Serbian military advisors headed by General Mile Mrkšić, a former commander of the JNA's special forces. Martić claims they were the first to abandon Knin, and that he, the president of Krajina, wasn't even informed of the attack and was practically ambushed in bed by the Croats. In a statement in the press, Martić said that it was obvious that Knin's capture had been allowed by Belgrade and that the JNA's withdrawal amounted to a transfer of Krajina to the Croats.

Milošević was told that Knin had fallen while he and his wife were relaxing in a Serbian mountain resort. People who spoke to him on the phone say that although he sounded shocked, he didn't say that Knin had "fallen" or was "captured," but rather "those imbeciles retreated," adding that the leaders of Krajina were "drunks" and "losers." His attitude set the tone in the media, and RTB didn't even interrupt its programming, upon which Patriarch Pavle wrote to its director, Milorad Vučelić, and sadly noted that Vučelić would be held accountable before "God and history."

On the evening of Knin's fall Milošević held separate meetings with the military leadership, newspaper editors he could trust, and the Socialist Party leadership. He didn't appear upset and said the fall of Knin was a consequence of the irrational policies of Martić and Karadžić. The press was instructed to blame them whenever they interviewed Krajinian refugees, and Serbs were so confused by the regime's propaganda that only a few hundred individuals, primarily Bosnian and Krajinian Serbs, gathered in front of the National Theatre to express their anger and accuse the leadership of treason.

The Croats proudly celebrated their great victory with toasts and bursts of gunfire, and their press compared Franjo Tudjman to Bismark, Churchill, and de Gaulle. While RTB announced that the defenders of Krajina were "regrouping," a helicopter carrying Tudjman landed in Knin's thirteenth-century fortress. Tudjman kissed the Croatian flag and announced, "On the eve of the new century, those who spread a cancer into Croatia have been routed. Upon military victories to be memorialized by a golden historical rubric, the foundations of an independant Croatia are finally in place."

Meanwhile, a fifty-kilometre-long column of refugees crawled along a highway in cars and trucks and horse-drawn trailers, on tractors and bicycles – anything on wheels. The refugees were terrified and depressed. Dust caked onto their sweat and their sunburns were only soothed by rain. Some slept in their ragged clothing in trailers and on horses, others sitting or standing, and all were going as far away from Krajina as possible. Some died from exhaustion while others gave birth. In despair a man killed his wife and two children before killing himself. Children were forced to take on adult responsibilities: nine-year-old Dejan Popović was seen behind the wheel of a Yugo, chauffeuring his mother, sister, grandmother, and a cousin with her baby, and another boy turned grey overnight.

When the refugees were interviewed, the word they used most frequently was "treason:"

Who is a traitor?
Everyone!
Who's everyone?
You in Belgrade.

Slobodan Milošević?
Him, it's him! He was a saint to us, a god, and now he's the Devil!
And Martić?
He's small potatoes, we all know that. The culprits are in Belgrade.
And General Mrkšić?
You people in Belgrade sent Mrkšić. He's an idiot!

Another refugee made the following statement: "I'm getting more and more angry that we didn't have our own country, government, or army – nothing but a shameful power-struggle, looting, and deceit. During four years of war in Krajina, people smuggled, caroused, and got bored. No one was preparing for defence. If you only saw the weapons we left behind, and we were routed like cattle!"

Croatia got rid of its Serbs in a day. Knin was left intact, as though residents had agreed to move out, and the Croats who would inhabit the city had everything they needed on site. Prior to the assault 300,000 Serbs had already left Croatia, and another 200,000 left upon Knin's fall.

Even Ante Pavelić, ustaša leader during World War II, hadn't achieved as much in the notorious Jasenovac concentration camp or the Bosnian mineshafts where countless Serbs, Jews, and Roma (gypsies) were thrown to their deaths. The Croatian Serbs had been promised independence, but Belgrade and Knin treasonously abetted Tudjman. Croatia was ultimately cleansed of its Serbs, thus bringing to fruition German Foreign Minister Klaus Kinkel's suggestion that Serbia be "brought to her knees."

Decked out in one of his beloved ceremonial uniforms, Tudjman beamingly announced that all participants in the operations in Slavonia were to receive honours. Croatian propaganda boasted that the capture of these territories was the greatest defeat inflicted upon Serbs since Kosovo Polje – regardless of the fact there hadn't been a real war but rather a simple drumming-out of the helpless. It was obvious that it was all a lie in which Belgrade, Zagreb, Knin, Pale, and the international community had collaborated.

Tudjman had been elected to office in 1990 by invoking Croatia's ustaša past, which terrified the people of Knin, whose memories of the fascist regime were still alive. When Serb nationalism was awakened, Milošević made promises that inflamed passions and encouraged revolt. Belgrade armed the Krajinians and encouraged their belligerence, but when it realized that Serbia's own survival was at stake, its only way out was to capitulate and abandon Krajina.

Had different governments been in place in Belgrade, Zagreb, and Knin, Serb Krajina could perhaps have been saved. But in Zagreb, Tudjman said that "the meadows, mountains, and fields in Croatia were Croatian," and that Pavelić's Croatia had not been a mere "fascist and criminal puppet state" but rather an expression of the Croatian people's "historical suffering." Serbs were warned that there was nothing for them in Croatia; but in Knin, wary of such a future and carried away by their initial victories, they rejected compromise and yielded to bloodlust, which in the final analysis proved that they weren't intelligent enough to achieve independence.

When Knin fell, the international community relaxed. The Serbs had lost, and informed opinion throughout the West, which had always considered the Serbs to have been the sole aggressors, was indifferent to the largest exodus in recent memory. Except for a few isolated voices there was no compassion for the refugees. Feeling that Serbs had got what they deserved, the West secretly applauded the Croatian blitzkrieg. According to the *New York Times*, the world didn't wish to hear the laments of Serb mothers. A member of the clergy noted that if "200,000 birds had been driven out of Krajina, worldwide opinion would have condemned such cruelty."

Milošević encouraged the Croatian Serbs throughout the war but purportedly agreed during a secret meeting with Franjo Tudjman on 25 March 1991 to let Croatia have its Serb-populated regions. According to Stipe Mesić, the regions were ceded in exchange for non-intervention in Serbia's plans to appropriate two-thirds of Bosnia. Tudjman's chief of staff, Hrvoje Šarinić, added that Milošević had told him that neither Serbia nor Croatia would allow Bosnia to remain intact, despite the Americans' "ignorant support" of Bosnia's Alia Izetbegović.

Milošević and Tudjman got along splendidly during the war. Though Tudjman frequently railed against "Serbo-Communist aggression," he never attacked or even mentioned Milošević, who in turn never denounced him. Warren Zimmerman has written that Tudjman told him he trusted Milošević, and that in private they addressed each other as "Franjo" and "Slobo." They kept in touch through Šarinić, who made thirteen visits to Belgrade between 1993 and 1999. Šarinić has said that Serbia's president wasn't at all concerned about Krajina, telling him, "When all's said and done, you'll get everything you want; but you're in too big of a rush, my friend." And though Milošević browbeat Šarinić, he showed genuine concern for Tudjman's health and told Šarinić that he was glad to hear that "Franjo" had pulled through a bout of illness.

Tudjman was a horrendous chauvinist, while Milošević simply lusted for power, but they were nonetheless similar in that they were both autocrats inclined to take political risks. Their backgrounds were also similar, in that Milošević's parents had committed suicide and Tudjman's father, Stjepan, murdered his wife before he committed suicide.

Krajina was betrayed well before it fell, and everything that happened in between was a mere political charade. Milošević encouraged the Croatian Serbs, even though he had already yielded to Tudjman, and told Šarinić that the only obstacle to his recognition of Croatia was Krajina. Referring to Cyprus, where "the Turks set up a border that can no longer be removed," Milošević then duped Ćosić into believing that Krajina would achieve independence. What really mattered to Milošević was avoiding personal humiliation. He betrayed Krajina because he was more easily reconciled to its military defeat than to Serbia's, over which he would have had to preside. As people in Zagreb readily affirm, General Mrkšić was sent to Krajina to execute this betrayal.

Tudjman proceeded with the invasion of Krajina – "Operation Hurricane," as it was known – without assuming any risk. He knew the JNA wouldn't intervene, and meanwhile, the Americans, quoting Franklin Roosevelt, acknowledged that for the time being Tudjman was their "son-of-a-bitch" and gave him the go-ahead, which included more support than anyone but the Germans had made available, including diplomatic assistance and intelligence and the bombardment of Krajina's electrical installations. After the invasion U.S. Defense Secretary William Perry was actually decorated by Tudjman, and in light of such tremendous support it comes as no surprise that Tudjman had confidently told Paddy Ashdown, the leader of the British Labour Party, that the whole operation would be over within ten days. Ten days? It was all over in seventeen hours!

Serbia looked upon Krajina's fall and the subsequent exodus of its inhabitants as though it were a minor setback. No diplomatic measures of any consequence were taken, and the impoverished refugees, who no longer even had the right to a free coffin, were callously ignored. Tudjman wouldn't have them, and Serbia's reserves were so low it couldn't provide for even its own people. Ordinary citizens of Serbia, who were hardly responsible for the refugees' plight and had many problems of their own, were the only ones who showed any compassion. Cohabitation with Serbs was no longer an issue in Croatia, and a Serb dream ended in despair.

Meanwhile, in spite of the refugees' suffering, humiliation, and sense of abandonment, Serbian propaganda insisted they must never forget the help they received from the government. Miloševic stated that "the solidarity of the Serbian people" was the most "beautiful testimonial to their humanitarian nature" and that "all those who benefited ... must remember it as a moral lesson, and also a debt they might well be asked to repay to a future generation" of Serbs. Markovic went even further. Writing about the Serbian people's generosity, she bitterly accused the opposition of stirring up resentment among the refugees and setting them against their benefactors in government who had not only provided them "with a home, food, clothing, and other necessities but ... saved their lives." Markovic concluded that "to incite unemployed refugees who have no means of subsistence, and are often literally without food or clothing, to rise against those who have given them everything, is a dishonesty of biblical proportions."

Though the Serbs had been defeated, Miloševic had once again emerged victorious. His leadership was now secure, he had the respect and backing of the West, and the Serbian media referred to him as "the world's foremost peacemaker." On 7 August 1996 he and Tudjman met in Athens to sign an agreement by which Yugoslavia and Croatia would formally recognize each other. The Serbian president had been cruising the Aegean on a yacht with his wife and daughter, and two days earlier, on the anniversary of Knin's fall, Tudjman announced that at the dawn of the second millennium Krajina was "back in the arms of Croatia, as pure as it was in King Zvonimir's time."

12

Glory in Defeat

On 21 November 1995 in Dayton, Ohio, after three weeks of round-the-clock negotiations, or rather, after three weeks of captivity, Milošević, Tudjman, and Izetbegović reached an agreement and finally put an end to the greatest slaughter continental Europe had witnessed since World War II. They were exhausted, but confident that they had acted in the best interests of their people. Milošević, the most despised statesman of the 1990s, was the star of the Dayton conference and received the heartiest applause.

Without the intervention of the White House, there would not have been an agreement, yet without the Serbian president's determination to end the war there would have been no triumph for the Clinton administration. Milošević understood that his fate was in the hands of the world's greatest power and agreed to everything they wanted. The central figure in Dayton was Richard Holbrooke, the foremost representative of a new and abrasive diplomatic style, behind which stands enormous, unhesitating clout. Holbrooke is a former attorney who knows how to deal with tyrants and bullies, and he wielded a mace. In 1992 he had stated that Milošević was becoming "Europe's most bloody tyrant," but now that they were engaged in negotiations, they exchanged compliments and the kind of jokes diplomatic manners usually prohibit. In the alluringly crude manner of powerful individuals, Holbrooke dispensed with formality and got results by telling his counterparts whenever they departed from the agenda that there had been enough "bullshit" and "historical lectures."

Pressured by the international community and broken by internal strife, Serbia had no other way out. Knin had been lost, and while Serbs in Croatia were being persecuted, those in Bosnia were barely surviving. Having claimed 70 per cent of the former Bosnian Republic's territory, the Bosnian Serbs came close to achieving independence but then nearly lost everything when NATO began to bombard them. In more than three thousand sorties, the western alliance damaged the Serbs' military potential far more significantly than had been acknowledged, and the balance of power subsequently shifted in favour of the Muslims and Croats. Banja Luka became helpless and nearly fell when most of its inhabitants abandoned the city to retreat from the Muslim and Croat assault. Fortunately it was saved through diplomatic means when the Americans, fearing the war would spread, decided that there had been enough fighting.

Milošević knew the war was lost and finally turned to diplomacy. Having abandoned his heroic posturing, he blamed everything on Karadžić. Though Karadžić and the Pale leadership had done their best to resist Milošević's attempts to pressure them, they could ultimately not get by without him. Upon meeting with him in the presence of Patriarch Pavle (whose popularity both sides exploited in order to lessen the impact of the unpalatable surrender), Karadžić, who was wanted by the International War Crimes Tribunal in The Hague, relinquished his right to represent the Bosnian Serbs in Dayton. A delegation of Bosnian Serbs travelled to Ohio, but their presence was merely symbolic. Milošević contemptuously told Holbrooke to disregard them, and though their future was being determined, no one even asked for their opinions.

Milošević's attitude towards the Americans was completely different. While he was usually either harsh and unyielding or deliberately confounding and obscure, he was extremely pleasant in Dayton. When negotiations were at an impasse, he managed to get them moving again by making light of himself, and the foreign press, which had always portrayed him as a hostile and dishonest politician, saw that he could relax, be witty, and engage in pleasant conversation. His upbeat mood in Dayton was fuelled by alcohol, as he was generally inclined to brace himself with a few drinks when under pressure.

Given more persistence, he could have avoided sharing control of the town of Brčko, but he came to fancy himself a conciliator and made bigger concessions than Izetbegović was ready to make. Besides Brčko and Goradže, the biggest issue was Sarajevo. The Americans hadn't expected that Serbia would accept losing the capital city to Bosnia, and Milošević could at least have obtained concessions regarding the policing of areas under Pale's control. Astonishingly, he made no demands to that effect, and Izetbegović and Prime Minister Haris Silajdžić have claimed that he told them they deserved Sarajevo because, while "those cowards [the Bosnian Serbs] were raining death on their people" they had "fought for Sarajevo." Even Bill Clinton was surprised to hear that Milošević hadn't made a fuss over the Muslims' demands for outright control of the city and praised his "sobriety." When an agreement was finally reached, Holbrooke cheerfully opened a bottle of wine, and all the war's victims were forgotten in a toast.

On 22 November 1995, Milošević returned from Dayton with the confidence that emanates only from the victorious. At the airport he was welcomed by his wife, daughter, and son, as well as the nation's ranking officials. It was an exceptional opportunity for reporters and cameramen, because it was the first time his wife had both sent him off on a trip and welcomed him back. The rest of the world saw Dayton as a victory for Tudjman and Izetbegović, but in Belgrade, it was Milošević who was celebrated. Wartime exuberance gave way to celebrations of peace, which the media and Socialist Party encouraged. Slobodan wasn't just the saviour of Serbia; he had also recaptured the international community's respect!

During election campaigns in 1992 the Socialist Party's leading slogans had been Milošević's exhortations to the nation: "Serbia will not yield to international sanctions." "Serbia will not give in, but will face up to the world." "Serbia can endure a thousand years of sanctions." But now, after Dayton, the party's most powerful argument was the lifting of sanctions in the wake of an economic blockade that had lasted close to three and a half years.

There was peace, but the war had scarred the nation's soul. After a three-year siege no one could reassure Sarajevan Serbs that they would again be able to live among their Muslim and Croat neighbours. More than seventy thousand Serbs moved out of

districts controlled by Izetbegović's government, taking everything, including their ancestors' remains and church bells, with
them. The inhabitants of the village of Blažuj all attended a service
that was to be the last for many among them who had chosen to
leave, and quite a few of those who remained came to regret their
decision. Revenge was a reality, the inevitable consequence of the
insane war, and Serbs were paid back for what they had done to
the Muslims. Milošević wasn't altogether impervious to these
issues, but they didn't threaten his hold on power. Thanks to Dayton, and the new-found support of the West, he felt he could
easily restore his house to order.

However, when YUL arrived on the political scene, the Socialist
Party's prospects changed dramatically, as did Milošević's attitude toward the West. During its first years in existence the
Socialist Party was extremely powerful. Even the former Communists, supported by the JNA, couldn't match their level of organization and influence, and Tito himself never had as much control
over his citizens as Milošević's Socialists did. But the Socialist
Party was shaken from its roost by YUL, which quickly established
itself as the most influential Serbian party.

Suddenly "the regime" no longer referred to the Socialists but
to YUL, even though it was in fact a minority party. Milošević went
along with this and became more involved in his wife's party than
in his own. Marković and other founders of YUL had provoked
rifts within the Socialist Party by suggesting it was divided into
nationalist and leftist camps, hawks and doves. Among the
nationalist hawks, the most prominent were ranking members of
the Socialist Party, including Professor Mihajlo Marković, Borisav
Jović, and Milorad Vučelić, all bitterly opposed to Marković's new
party. Their polemic lasted a few weeks and provided much
entertainment in the press.

Milošević didn't get involved. Mihajlo Marković, the Socialists'
leading ideologue, had already compromised himself by continu-
ing to support the Bosnian Serbs, and so Milošević, as was usually
the case when an associate was no longer useful to him, allowed
his wife to finish him off. When Mihajlo Marković suggested that
YUL wasn't a credible party, Mirjana Marković replied that he was
merely a "decrepit academician and infantile Socialist" who had
"slobbered his way through allegiances to the partisans, Commu-

nists, Praxis [former Yugoslavia's academic incarnation of the 1960s' new left], and the nationalist movement."

Borisav Jović fell into a trap of his own making. Following the 8th Plenary Session, Milošević, thinking Jović would know which side his bread was buttered on, promoted him to the most important post in Serbian government, namely Serbia's seat in the Yugoslav Presidency. But Jović became daringly high-minded during his short tenure as president of the Socialist Party and actually challenged Milošević's supremacy in an exchange that was carried by the press. It began when Milošević, referring to Jović, denounced the arrogance and vanity of "certain members of the leadership."

Jović's career was hanging by a single thread, which came loose when his account of former Yugoslavia's breakdown was published. Jović scrutinized his past with uncompromising and even merciless probity, as a man who had either decided to purge his conscience or simply wasn't aware of the implications of his many disclosures. In any case, his longstanding devotion to public service was sufficient proof that he had acted in the public's best interests. His book was a devastating and horrifying account of the leadership's ineptitude and corruption.

Milorad Vučelić was another member of the Socialist leadership ousted by Milošević. Belonging to a younger generation of intellectuals in whom the public had placed its hopes for a democratic future, Vučelić had participated in the 1968 movement for reform and was a pro-Yugoslav democrat until the mid-1980s when he embraced Dobrica Ćosić's brand of nationalism. During the 8th Plenary Session and immediately thereafter, Vučelić criticized Milošević but then embraced his policies upon Ćosić's recommendation. Vučelić's power was further enhanced when he became majority leader in the Serbian parliament, and was appointed to run the Serbian state television. He wielded a big axe and fired one hundred television employees deemed disloyal or critical towards Milošević's political line.

With Dayton behind him, Milošević was able to proceed with his purge of the Socialist Party leadership. On 28 November 1995 the party's executive committee assembled. Though Milošević was greeted by a standing ovation, he had come to despise his function

as president of the Socialist Party, and having announced that the
party's next congress was to be promoted as "Serbia 2000: A Step
into the New Century," he summarily enumerated his latest
victims: Borisav Jović, Mihajlo Marković, and Milorad Vučelić
were dismissed from the party's executive committee, and the
leaders of the Belgrade and Novi Sad committees, Slobodan
Jovanović and Radovan Pankov, were also relieved of their duties.
The entire meeting lasted seventeen minutes, upon which Milošević cheerfully invited everyone to join him for a drink in honour
of the Dayton accord.

No one had been informed of the impending purge. Mihajlo
Marković was told as he was packing for a trip to Greece that a
meeting had been called, and a reporter with Radio B-92 unwit-
tingly told Jović that he had been ousted when she called him to
ask for his comments.

The Socialist Party's congress, held on 2 March 1996, was also a
hasty affair. Within a few hours the new leadership was introduced, and the "triumph of peace on the eve of the twenty-first
century" was celebrated. The ugly past was forgotten, and many
promises were made. Mirjana Marković didn't attend, but neither
did her enemies in the leadership, who had all been replaced by
her minions or by allies of Milošević of whom she approved. YUL,
a party without a single representative in parliament, had taken
over Serbia's leading institution. Furthermore, Marković had been
telling her associates that Milošević was "tired," thereby implying
that she was in charge. Whether the Serbian president had in fact
endorsed his wife's ambition to succeed him remains unclear, but
in any case the press was soon behaving as though he had.

13

Lords of the Press

The regime never relinquished its control of the media, but it did loosen its grip whenever it felt it was politically expedient to do so. Such "liberalizations" were only meant to appease the public, and editors who ran afoul of the regime during these periods of so-called reform were invariably replaced by ever more docile individuals recruited from the profession's dregs. RTB and *Politika* spearheaded government propaganda and became the moral and professional graveyards of Serbian journalism.

After the 8th Plenary Session RTB became the foremost disseminator of the regime's propaganda. It was the first to engage in any battle and worked systematically to consolidate the regime. Deeply involved in all major political upheavals, it provoked many of Belgrade's most massive demonstrations. Not surprisingly, its facilities were more heavily guarded than the JNA's headquarters, and when the first anniversary of the March 1991 demonstrations approached, no political or military means were spared to ensure its protection.

While Milošević was probably more involved in minutiae than any autocrat in recent memory and certainly had a hand in his government's control of the media, his wife eventually became their overlord. Marković enjoyed the coverage she received, and as an author whose lofty works appeared in the press, she believed she was a more qualified arbiter than her husband, and took over from him in the mid-1990s. Editors who cared for their jobs were suddenly more mindful of her opinions than they were of her husband's, and she developed a loyal coterie of journalists who were almost like children to her and were therefore more secure in their positions than anyone else. On the other hand, anyone who opposed her was labelled a corrupt traitor, and her party's program stated that the independent media were "standard-bearers in a war more dangerous than conventional warfare."

The Miloševićs worked together closely, but their relationship was competitive and often included minor slights as comical as they were harmful to their reputations. Though they endlessly subverted each other's authority, it was hard to tell whether they were seriously at each other's throats or simply diverting themselves for lack of anything better to do. Often, their quarrels were about whose favourites would get government jobs, or who their next victim would be. Such disputes were at times dramatic, but as the careers of two of Serbia's most influential journalists demonstrate, Marković usually got her way.

Hadji Dragan Antić is unmatched in the annals of Serbian journalism for demonstrating the perverse effects of a virtually instantaneous rise to power. In the 1970s people entered journalism with either a university degree or strong political connections. Antić had neither, and began at *Politika* as a freelancer. Unable to choose his assignments, he did a bit of everything and ranked among the lowly reporters who were in fact the heart and soul of the editorial staff. Young, enterprising, and sociable Antić soon had a wide circle of friends. He endeared himself to Belgrade intellectuals and established a close rapport with dissidents. In the mid-1980s his interview with Milovan Djilas, the Tito era's foremost dissident, was published and he entered into the confidence of the church – remarkable feats, considering that both Djilas and the church were heavily censured at the time.

Antić's career took an ominous turn when he befriended Milošević's daughter, Marija, who provided him with an entrée into the world of politics and finance. Marija was smitten by Antić and introduced him to her family, where he was treated not only with respect but as an intimate. He quickly became the Miloševićs' closest friend, advisor, and leading propagandist. Suddenly he found himself at the helm of *Politika*, wielding powers that even the Ribnikars, who had founded the paper, never had. He was accountable to no one but himself, and given his new-found connections, no one dared question his authority. He decided what went into the paper, reprimanded and bestowed lavish rewards on employees, and generally behaved as though he owned *Politika*, the Balkans' largest publishing house. His new stature required new friendships with high-ranking politicians and entrepreneurs, and all the accoutrements of power, including bodyguards.

His ascent was closely related to Živorad Minović's fall. Minović was a shrewd, capable, and independently minded professional. He, along with General Ljubičić, Mirjana Marković, and Dušan Mitević, had helped Milošević take over during the 8th Plenary Session, upon which Minović then became Serbian nationalism's leading propagandist; however he was convinced that the regime would collapse following the March 1991 demonstrations and began to support Vuk Drašković. When Milošević overcame that crisis, Minović realized that he had bitten off more than he could chew and returned to his old allegiances. Milošević forgave him but didn't forget, and kept him in check by having Antić promoted as managing editor. A debilitating struggle ensued between the two newsmen, who divided *Politika*'s staff into bitterly opposed factions, each with their own security staff and firearms, which during the 1990s had become status symbols among reporters.

Before going to Dayton, Milošević told Marković he didn't have the energy to fire Minović and would take care of him upon his return. Marković couldn't wait and had him fired while Milošević was away.

14

The Mighty Opposition

The Socialists won virtually all Serbian elections throughout the 1990s. Though they obviously engaged in fraud, they would have won even if they hadn't. Their success lay in Milošević's cleverness and in the gullibility of an electorate which, despite having been deceived on numerous occasions, continued to believe him.

When the opposition was legalized, Dragoljub Mićunović's Democratic Party appeared to be the most promising new party. Mićunović, a cheerful former dissident who was among a group of philosophers expelled from Belgrade University during the mid-1970s, brought many esteemed intellectuals and independent thinkers into his party's ranks, including writers, academicians, and other former dissidents. However, petty quarrels dissipated the leadership, and the party eventually splintered into four smaller entities, precipitating Serbia's calamitous decline. Together they could have presented an alternative to the regime, but divided as they were, they only managed to upset the already confused electorate.

The Democratic Party's largest offshoot continued to be known as the Democratic Party and was taken over by Zoran Djindjić. But Djindjić, an eloquent man who studied at the University of Heidelberg and tirelessly pursued his political aspirations, was an unreliable ally. Prone to engage in brazen one-upmanship and deceit, he frequently changed his mind and once even withdrew from elections in the midst of a campaign. Despite numerous adamantly reformist platforms, his party never accomplished much and posed no threat to the regime.

Vojislav Koštunica, the leader of the Democratic Party of Serbia, was also amongst the expelled Belgrade University professors. Initially greeted as a potential unifier of the opposition, he insisted that his party remain ideologically pure. Unable to enter into working relationships with potential allies, he went his own way and assumed the role of a solitary guardian of morality who worked against the regime and the other members of the opposition.

The Democratic Party's two other off-shoots found themselves in a similar situation. Professor Nikola Milošević and Kosta Čavoški, the leaders of the Liberal Party, were intense critics of the regime but paid no attention to the electorate, and Dragoljub Mičunović's Democratic Centre turned into a debating society for genteel opponents of the regime.

Altogether, close to 130 parties were formed in Serbia, but only a few meant anything, having either drawn a substantial following of their own or thanks to influential allies. For instance, Dušan Mihajlović's New Democracy benefited from a succession of alliances with Dobrica Čosić, Vuk Drašković, and Milošević, and Vesna Pešić's Civic Alliance consistently opposed the war, and therefore benefited from western support. However, the vast majority of these parties were led by individuals whose sole interest was to collect scraps of privilege, and thus they warrant no further mention.

Besides YUL and the Socialists, the political tone was set by Vuk Drašković's SRM and Vojislav Šešelj's Radical Party. Šešelj was Serbia's most fanatical nationalist, a rabid anti-communist who could neither be cajoled, bribed, or threatened into submission by the regime. However, he endorsed Milošević when Milošević embraced nationalism, and later only withdrew his support when it would have hindered Milošević. Šešelj didn't shy away from criminal behaviour and landed in prison a few times, first in his native Bosnia, where he endured a particularly harsh sentence before being forced into exile, and later in Serbia. Seeking revenge, he built a political base among disenfranchised Serbs in Vojvodina and Serbia and was the first to send paramilitaries into Bosnia. With support from the regime, he became a Vojvodinian representative in Yugoslavia's parliament in the early 1990s and repaid his debt many times over by wreaking havoc within the opposition.

Šešelj openly endorsed ethnic cleansing during the war and travelled around Vojvodina with a list of Croats he claimed were proven enemies of Serbia. Needless to say, his actions were harmful to Serbia, contributing greatly to the notion that all Serbs were bloodthirsty fiends who went about clenching daggers between their teeth. Šešelj would even show up in parliament wearing combat fatigues but renounced them when he was told they made him look like a pregnant frog. His fanaticism was unpalatable to Milošević, but Milošević needed his support to have Čosić impeached and so endorsed him, stating that he respected Šešelj because he felt that he and his party were "financially independent from the West, and ideologically consistent." Still, Šešelj provided his detractors with evidence of insanity on a daily basis, and no one, not even the electorate, was safe from his provocations. He called Drašković's SRM the "Serbian Illusion Movement," announced when NATO squadrons based in Italy bombarded the Bosnian Serbs that he would follow "Nero's historical example" and set fire to Rome, and stated that as long as there were "imbeciles in Serbia," his political career was safe.

His anti-communism irked Marković, but she refrained from attacking him while Milošević needed his support and only went into action when Milošević became a "peacemaker." On 28 September 1993 the government issued a statement accusing Šešelj of being a "fascist criminal of war" who "personifies violence and promotes hatred," a "political monster," a "primitive nationalist," a "common criminal," and last but not least, a "two-bit politician from Sarajevo who has abused Belgrade's hospitality." The statement was obviously written by Marković, who wrote for the government whenever she felt the occasion warranted her input.

Benefiting from the Serbs' disapproval of Marković's involvement in government affairs, Šešelj mounted an obscenity-ridden campaign in which he frequently suggested that Milošević was henpecked by Marković. On one occasion during an appearance on *Politika*'s televized news hour, he suggested that Marković wasn't really a woman. *Politika*'s directors were horrified and banned him from all of their forums, but Tomislav Nikolić, his second-in-command, took up the slack. Nikolić's devastating arguments, delivered in a calm tone of voice, wreaked havoc among his opponents. He came across like a pathologist performing an autopsy, and stated, for example, that "Milošević can allow himself to be henpecked at home, but not in the Republic of Serbia."

Members of Šešelj's party were forcibly removed from parliament upon having similarly insulted Marković, and on 18 June 1994, after he vandalized microphone cables in parliament, Šešelj was called before the court. He told the judge he had a statement to make for the record. "Mr Judge," he said, "all I can say in my defence is that Slobodan Milošević is Serbia's biggest criminal."

Milošević didn't stoop to his level and regretted that his wife was being insulted on his account. But Marković was entirely in her element. She replied that Šešelj was a "primitive Turk who is afraid to fight like a man, and instead sits around insulting other men's wives."

Šešelj was a hard nut to crack, and wherever he went (which seemed to be everywhere), he continued to insult Marković. In medieval times such conflicts would have ended in duels, and heads would have rolled, but what awaited Šešelj was prison. All that was needed was a good reason to send him there, and there were plenty of those. He continued to attack the Miloševićs and disrupted parliament throughout the summer. His parliamentary immunity was revoked in mid-September, when he received a three-year sentence for having destroyed government property. A few days later he spat in the Commons leader's face. Arrested the following day, he was handed an additional thirty-day sentence and sent to jail. Released after having served three months, his first statement was "Slobodan Milošević is a communist bandit." Having once spent twenty-one months in a Bosnian prison for assault, Šešelj was not intimidated and later said that the only thing that would stop him would be a bullet to the head.

There was no end to these skirmishes between Šešelj and the regime. He and Nikolić soon spent two months in jail for violating the regime's ban on public gatherings, but as their attacks focused on Marković, Milošević was increasingly seen as a victim of his own inability to control his ambitious wife. However, one needn't rush to conclusions. A run-down moral climate ensured that nothing was permanent in Serbia, least of all friendship and enmity.

Vuk Drašković had been a problem for Milošević since his early
days in power. A gifted charismatic speaker, he was a wizard in
the eyes of many of Serbia's people. He had trained as a lawyer,
and before Yugoslavia's breakup worked as a journalist, supporting the regime in articles he would later regret. He then tried his
hand at the arts and courageously wrote several novels dealing
with human rights abuses under the communists and the persecution of Serbs during World War II. However, he truly thrived
upon entering politics, where his charisma and talent for stirring a
crowd into a belligerent frenzy drew a wide following among
relatively young and fanatical monarchists. Much like Šešelj, he
demanded that all territories that had belonged to Serbia in 1918,
when the Kingdom of Serbs, Croats, and Slovenes was established, be returned to Serbia. He also sent paramilitary units into
Bosnia and Croatia during the war and boasted that he would be
able to provide a new Serbian army with sixty thousand volun-
teers. Though Drašković was not personally a violent man and
suffered a great deal whenever he harmed anyone, his ambitions
were overriding, and both he and others were often confounded
by their magnitude.

In parliament on 1 June 1994 a Radical Party member assaulted
one of Drašković's associates. Drašković and his wife, Danica,
gathered their followers that evening in protest. Danica Drašković
incited the crowd to riot, and a police officer was severely beaten
and later died. Shortly after midnight police raided their headquarters. Calling Mrs Drašković a "barren whore," they arrested
and beat the couple, and a motion was subsequently entered to
abolish their party.

Drašković was as devoted to his wife – a Montenegrin mountain girl who had worked as a prosecutor in a municipal court
under the communists – as Milošević was to Marković, and
successfully appealed to Marković to have her released from
prison. But he himself remained incarcerated and underwent
surgery as a result of injuries sustained during his arrest. Subsequently he went on a hunger strike, and an international outcry
ensued during which Patriarch Pavle, Simon Wiesenthal, François
Mitterand, and countless others appealed to Milošević to set him
free. Milošević refused, and when Mitterand's wife appealed to
him in person, stating that Drašković's life was in danger, Miloše-

vić informed her that Drašković was healthy enough to be spending entire days playing chess.

Drašković announced that he would die on 17 July 1994, the anniversary of the executions of Russia's last Czar and Draža Mihajlović, leader of the chetnik movement during World War II. But after he called for Bishop Artemije to perform his last rites, Drašković was released, and many Serbs felt that Milošević's crack-down had backfired. However, incarceration had a profound effect on Drašković. He endorsed Milošević's turnaround and began to criticize nationalists who refused to accept the unconditional surrender of Bosnian Serbs. Then, pandering to the West, with whose support he believed he would overthrow the regime, Drašković declared that Milošević had merely adopted his views. Most of his party's leaders subsequently abandoned him, and many of its members followed suit.

In March 1995 Mirjana Marković approached Drašković on Milošević's behalf and offered him the vice-presidency of Serbia in exchange for his support in parliament. Confident that he would win the presidency in upcoming elections and unwilling to accept a secondary role, Drašković refused, and his wife accused the Miloševićs of attempting to shore up their crumbling regime at her husband's expense. As elections approached, a riotous exchange ensued in the press between Danica Drašković and Marković, in which the former was accused of being a "semi-savage goatherd" and the latter a "schizophrenic epileptic."

15

Egg on Your Face

As governor of the central bank, Dragoslav Avramović had saved Yugoslavia from hyperinflation and wanted to liberalize the economy. Dismissed for having revealed that government ministers were lining their pockets, he continued to criticize the regime and accepted the leadership of Together, the opposition's newly formed coalition. His candidacy would have been a threat to Milošević, but he abruptly withdrew. Some suggested that he was being blackmailed or otherwise threatened by the regime.

Though shrill propaganda suggested that Yugoslavia's survival depended on the regime's victory, Milošević didn't bother to campaign in person. His confidence was vindicated on 3 November 1996 when the regime obtained sixty-six seats in the federal parliament against the opposition's twenty-two. "The opposition has collapsed and will never come to power," he told the leadership. He was convinced that the regime would easily win the next round of municipal elections, which were to be held on 17 November. But when the results came in, the opposition had taken Belgrade and thirty-three urban municipalities, representing 50 per cent of the population. It was a substantial defeat for Milošević and didn't bode well for Serbia's upcoming parliamentary election.

Milošević blamed his campaign managers but otherwise seemed to accept defeat and said it wasn't a problem for him because it wouldn't affect his control of foreign policy and would also teach his people a lesson. However, ranking officials, wary of being swept from office, convinced him that the opposition's victory would carry over into the Serbian election. Milošević then gathered his campaign managers and told them to cheer up, a reassurance that became more meaningful later that night when the previous day's returns were falsified. According to a witness, the judge who directed the fraud was so zealous that he could have, had he been asked, simultaneously overturned the results of the Romanian elections and the U.S. elections being held at roughly the same time.

The government expected that weary Serbs would be indifferent to the "final tally," but the proverbial cup was full, and demonstrations that began in Kragujevac quickly spread to all municipalities in which the opposition had won. In Belgrade between 100,000 and 200,000 demonstrators gathered each day. Drašković called for the opposition's victory to be defended "at all costs," and Zoran Djindjić suggested demonstrators arm themselves with raw eggs. Media and government headquarters were subsequently pelted by angry demonstrators, but when students joined the protests, the demonstrators' rage gave way to a carnival atmosphere. Whistles and rattleboxes, drums, pots and pans, trumpets, horns, and cowbells were carried into the streets, and columns of demonstrators from all walks of life and political affiliations, including members of the Socialist Party, held their noses while passing in front of media headquarters. On the following day the "Serbian Airforce" was engaged, and thousands of paper airplanes were launched at RTB's studios in eerie anticipation of 1999's attack by NATO warplanes.

At the end of each day marchers gathered in Belgrade's Republic Square, where Drašković, Djindjić, and Vesna Pešić, who appeared only together, encouraged their peaceful tactics. At 7:30 P.M. when the evening news was aired, residents set their stereo speakers at their windows to "drown out the lies."

Meanwhile Marković was on a seven-day tour of India, promoting her most recent literary effort. She and Milošević spoke daily but, not wishing to upset her, he underplayed the magnitude of the demonstrations. After New Delhi she headed to Jaipur, a city she would vividly recall for an encouraging episode regarding her political future. She and her entourage visited an astrologer who worked in their hotel. In a turban and a long beard, sitting cross-legged and utterly absorbed in his thoughts, he inspired their trust. He revealed that Mirjana had been born in a forest and said that her political star would shine for another ten years.

Professor Markovic was impressed and did not regret the thirty-five dollars she had spent on the reading.

Miloševic greeted his wife at the airport on 30 November 1996, barely able to conceal his concern. Markovic was shocked by the state of affairs in Serbia and immediately called a series of meetings with her associates.

In Požarevac the Miloševics' son, Marko, stormed into the studios of Bum 93, a radio station that had reported on the demonstrations. He went straight to the station manager's office and, keeping one hand behind his back on the pommel of his gun, spewed a torrent of threats and obscenities in which he accused the manager of being a corrupt traitor. He then angrily lined up the station's staff. "Do you know what's in store for you?" he shouted. "Do you want me to tear out your antennas, destroy your equipment, and see to it that within two hours your station's shut down? I'll show you who you're fucking with!" And indeed he did, for Bum 93 was subsequently banned for eight months.

The demonstrations went on for weeks, and though it appeared that Miloševic would be the first autocrat to be felled by pots, pans, and whistles, he remained confident in his authority and refused even to address the demonstrators. The exception was a group of students who had walked from Nis to Belgrade, desperately claiming they had proof that the regime's victory was fraudulent. Citizens of Belgrade greeted them as heroes, and Miloševic agreed to receive them. Though he chastized them for promoting the rule of foreign interests, his eyes betrayed that he was extremely ill at ease. Miloševic then assured the students that Serbia would not protect anyone who had broken its law.

The opposition appeared to be on the verge of a breakthrough, but Mirjana Markovic would not consider the possibility of defeat and accused them of being a "subversive, terroristic fifth column" that had "corrupted Serbia's youth." Miloševic then received the chair of the U.S. Committee to Protect Journalists, Kati Marton, and suggested that only a few thousand people were involved in the demonstrations, adding that the students were being manipulated by nationalist academics. Though his guest had hoped to discuss the matter further, Miloševic told her that he had to leave because he was going on a duck hunt.

U.S. Secretary of State Warren Christopher had already put pressure on Miloševic, stating that Serbs deserved a market economy, freedom of the press, and fair elections, just like their counterparts in former Eastern Blok countries. Milošević's associates suggested that the regime organize counter-demonstrations to show the "true face" of Serbia, and thus take a firm stand against Christopher. In a reply that Christopher received shortly before tendering his resignation, Milošević called the demonstrators "anti-democratic vandals" who were making "terroristic threats" and should therefore "not be supported by a democratic government." He approved counter-demonstrations, and telegrams and letters of support poured into his offices. Industrial managers sent telegrams on behalf of workers, farm managers on behalf of peasants, veterans' associations on behalf of veterans, and school principals on behalf of teachers. The same phrases were used over and over again, and the same faces kept appearing at counter-demonstrations throughout Belgrade.

More participants were brought in from surrounding cities following the Serbian government's announcement that a rally to end all rallies would be held in the heart of Belgrade, in the same location where the opposition's supporters usually gathered. It was a monstrous, potentially disastrous idea that no one believed until bleachers were erected. On 24 December 1996 trains and buses carrying Milošević's supporters poured into Belgrade. Placards bearing his likeness and slogans such as "Thanks for Dayton" and the ever-present "No Foreign Intervention" were handed out to nearly all participants, and everyone got a free lunch and leave with pay. Many were there because their superiors had ordered them to go, while others were bribed with cash or employment. Given their modest and worn attire (there were many Roma among them), it was apparent that most of them were poor and generally benefited the least from Milošević's regime. Jeers and insults greeted them throughout Belgrade, and a few heated exchanges with Milošević's Kosovar supporters almost ended in disaster.

Accompanied by occasional cries of "Arrest Drašković!" Milošević addressed the crowd in a manner that reminded a foreign observer of former Eastern-Blok dictators. He vowed that no one would "destabilize Serbia." When the rally ended, his supporters rushed back to their awaiting transportation.

While the official media claimed that 500,000 supporters of the regime had gathered, foreign intelligence estimates put numbers between 40,000 and 60,000. Meanwhile, one hundred metres away in Republic Square, Vuk Drašković, Zoran Djindjić, and Vesna Pešić held forth for the thirty-fifth consecutive day and drew a record-breaking crowd of 200,000 participants.

New Year's Eve turned into a magnificent outdoor celebration when 100,000 residents gathered in an unprecedented expression of solidarity, joy, and cathartic spirituality. Reporting from Belgrade, an Italian reporter was so moved that he wondered "where this beautiful, spiritual nation" had been hiding. Meanwhile, the Miloševićs were in Karadjordjevo, a hundred kilometres away. A power failure hit their area, and Marković, who thought it was the work of their enemies, had the entire upper management of Serbia's electrical utility fired.

Determined to put an end to the demonstrations, Milošević ordered police reinforcements to be sent to Belgrade. On 2 February a large contingent led by Drašković was dispersed with tear gas, water cannons, and clubs. Approximately two hundred people were injured, including Vesna Pešić, who was beaten as she was tending to a fallen demonstrator's injuries. It appeared that Milošević had decided it was time to crush the opposition – but as usual any rational attempt to evaluate his actions was off the mark. On 4 February there was sensational news. Milošević announced that a special law was being enacted to validate the original results of Serbia's municipal elections. Speaking as though he had had no part in the fiasco, he went on to say the electoral "dispute" had caused much damage to the country and that it was "finally time" to resolve the matter. Once again he showed that he was Serbia's sole master and could punish and reward as he saw fit.

On 21 February 1997, in celebration of Zoran Djindjić's inauguration as mayor of Belgrade, thousands of citizens gathered downtown one last time. Amid song, laughter, and flying bottles of beer, a pair of youths defied gravity and scaled the city hall to remove its communist star. However, no more than fifty metres away, its identical twin remained securely fastened to the presidential palace.

The Together coalition fell apart while demonstrators were still swollen from the beatings they had received from police. Drašković had entered the coalition and supported Djindjić's bid for

Belgrade's mayoralty under the condition that he be its leader and candidate in Serbia's next presidential election. But he also limited Djindjić's independence by ensuring that his own people were in control of the city's finances. Djindjić retaliated by withdrawing his support of Drašković's candidacy. They subsequently spent so much time hurling insults at each other that when water shortages hit Belgrade, many residents believed Mira Marković, who said the shortages were the "first obvious consequence of right-wing government in Yugoslavia's capital." Meanwhile, Šešelj's Radical Party descended on the coalition like hyenas, until it was in complete disarray. All the regime had to do was create a special department within Tanjug to track and report its opponents' shameless ineptitude.

While the opposition self-destructed, Milošević, whose second and last available term as Serbia's president was about to expire, secured his hold on the leadership by taking over the Yugoslav Presidency. His only obstacle was Montenegro, his ancestral homeland, where the Socialist leadership was divided. His allies suggested that if the Socialist Party failed to unanimously support his candidacy, the party would collapse and take down the entire Montenegrin leadership. The election was called as soon as Milošević had the Socialists' support and, just to make sure there would be no surprises, his leading allies in parliament personally made sure their members circled his name on their ballots, and Yugoslavia's citizens were only told about the election when Milošević had already become their president-elect.

To further guard against any surprises, Milošević was inaugurated 27 July 1997 just a few days after his ambush of the presidency, and whatever legitimacy he may have lacked was amply compensated for by reactivation of the pomp that had surrounded Tito. Despite Marković's claim that the happiest days of her life had been spent in a modest New Belgrade appartment, she eagerly embraced her new lifestyle. This demanded motorcades surrounding Tito's Mercedes limousine and the reactivation and reviewing of the cartoonish honour guard at Belgrade's White Palace, a fabled edifice built for the Karadjordjevićs and preserved by former Yugoslavia's collective presidency as a relic of Tito.

Meanwhile doctors and industrial and utility workers who hadn't been paid in months demonstrated against the regime, alongside defrauded pensioners, refugees, and war veterans.

Omitting the kleptocracy, the only Serbs whose standard of living was improving were morticians, since about fifty refugees died of malnutrition or committed suicide each week. In an attempt to show that people were being taken care of, an RTB news crew reported from a soup kitchen operated by Belgrade's Red Cross. As many of the indigents turned their backs to the camera in shame, a portrait of Milošević came into focus so that viewers wouldn't forget whom the report's subjects had to thank for their meal. And when football matches between Serbian and Croatian teams resumed after a long hiatus, an RTB sportscaster assured viewers that the matches marked the "renewed peaceful collaboration between the peoples of Croatia and Serbia." Perhaps he was unaware that many of those he addressed were the homeless victims of Croatian ethnic cleansing.

16

Not a Chance

Serbian presidential elections were held during the autumn of 1997. Zoran Djindjić and Vesna Pešić boycotted them, but Drašković and Šešelj felt the road to the presidential palace was wide open and campaigned against Milošević's replacement, Zoran Lilić. Drašković's campaign promises often sounded as though he were hallucinating, especially when he announced that, thanks to the enormous respect he commanded in "Moscow, Rome, London, Paris, and New York," the nation's $9 billion debt would be written off as soon as he was elected. He also compared himself to Mike Tyson, until Tyson was knocked out, then proclaimed that he was Serbia's Peter the Great. His intrepid followers minted silver and gold coins bearing his likeness. Šešelj was more in tune with the electorate and promised he would prosecute criminals and recapture the nation's dignity. But though he beat Drašković and Lilić, he failed to obtain the required majority, and the election had to go into a second round.

Drašković refused to accept defeat. He blamed Djindjić, who had instigated the boycott, and told the foreign press that Djindjić was a warmonger who had opposed the Dayton conference. He then courted Šešelj, which involved agreeing with everything he said and posing with him for photographers in restaurants. Drašković also urged his wife, Danica, who had once challenged Šešelj to a duel, to greet his new ally politely.

On 30 September 1997, Drašković, backed by Šešelj and the Socialists, ousted Djindjić from city hall. Accusing Drašković of having betrayed the opposition, Djindjić and Pešić called a demonstration during which their followers chanted "Vuk and Slobo-dan, pushing daisies as one," and "Danice, Danice, Slobo's new fiancée." Though police attacked them so brutally that even innocent bystanders who had the misfortune of being in their path were injured, more demonstrations were called. Each time the marchers were again assaulted by police.

Meanwhile Milošević went to Greece a couple of times, cruis-ing the Aegean and visiting his well-heeled Athenian friends. Lilić's defeat wasn't a problem, since the alliance between Draško-vić and Šešelj fell apart as soon as Drašković assumed control of Belgrade. As well, the regime's second-round candidate, Yugosla-via's foreign affairs minister, Milan Milutinović, one of few ranking officials who hailed from a well-established family (his father was an engineer and his mother an art historian), was more respected than Lilić. What's more, the returns could always be adjusted.

Milošević and Milutinović had gone to law school together but only became close when Milutinović was appointed ambassador to Greece in the early 1990s, a post he remained in for two years into his tenure as minister of foreign affairs, purportedly because of his involvement with Milošević's alleged investments in Greece. A typically smooth *apparatchik*, he was haughty towards underlings and of course adept at polishing apples. Nevertheless, he was the most capable and trustworthy official Milošević could have chosen. Šešelj's and Drašković's bar-room brawls had left Serbia with no other option, and Milutinović entered parliament as Serbia's new president – surrounded by bodyguards and unannounced. Šešelj, backed by an independent investigation, had claimed that 700,000 votes were stolen. Chairs in the parliament press centre were stacked and locked away, and Radicals jeeringly denounced Milutinović and his fellow Socialists as criminals. Undoubtedly there was fraud, and only 50 per cent of the elector-ate had voted, but since it was better to have Milutinović in the presidency than Šešelj, there was no further outcry.

Milošević's man was in, but his party hadn't had a majority in parliament since 1992 and needed to co-opt either Drašković or Šešelj. Both were eager, though Drašković more so than Šešelj, having acquired a taste for perks such as having a police escort and seeing demonstrations against him quashed. But an alliance with the ultranationalist Šešelj could only have compromised Milošević internationally, and so Drašković was the obvious choice.

Though his support had weakened considerably since his betrayal of the opposition in Belgrade, Drašković demanded half of Serbia's ministerial portfolios, a truce between right and left, the adoption of Serbian holidays and insignia instead of the communist ones Milošević still held on to, and outright control of RTB and *Politika*. The regime listened to Drašković, upon which he announced that a "historical agreement" in which the Socialist Party would be Serbia's "left hand, the Serbian Renewal Movement its right," was close at hand.

Drašković went early to his office on 23 March 1998 because the new government was to be formed that day and he was anxious to hear from Milošević. By the time he left late at night, he hadn't heard from Milošević, the Radical Party had obtained thirteen ministerial portfolios, and Šešelj was Serbia's new deputy prime minister.

17

Premeditated Murder

At this point one might ask whether the Miloševićs feared repri-
sals. Serbs know that revenge is a dish best eaten cold. They endure, wait, and then exact a cruel redress. Between the early nine-
teenth and twentieth centuries, two rival Serbian dynasties, the
Karadjordjes and the Obrenovićs, were plagued by revenge, and a
handful of their members were brutally murdered.

During the tenth anniversary of Milošević's rule, there were no
such attempts, nor were there any indications that revenge was in
the offing. Still, recalling an incident that occurred on 2 January
1988 when the brand-new tires of the Miloševićs' Audi exploded
en route to Belgrade, any whiff of conspiracy was thoroughly
looked into. Suspecting that the incident had been an assassination attempt by his opponents within the Serbian political establishment, Milošević had ordered an investigation, and security
concerns were used to justify his family's move to an exclusive
address. Two separate committees spent weeks on the matter, but
no conspiracy was uncovered either then or on numerous other
occasions when the Miloševićs felt their lives were in danger. And
though Zurich-based Albanian separatists did once place a
million-dollar bounty on Milošević's head, he and his family led a
secure existence. Milošević eventually became more concerned
about the ability of Serbia's police to uphold his regime than he
was about his personal security. As a paramilitary force, the police
were highly organized and capable of keeping up to 150,000
people under surveillance. The opposition claimed twice that
number, but in any case everything seemed to be under control.

However, during the so-called privatizations of the 1990s, Serbia resembled a criminal organization in which political parties, security forces, and the leadership systematically looted the state and robbed the public, casually dismissing their actions as unavoidable. At state borders, for instance, families reduced to small-time peddling were taken for everything they had, while truckloads of "ministerially approved" luxury goods were waved through without so much as a dinar being levied.

On 20 February 1997 a thirty-nine-year-old bully named Vladan Kovačević was murdered in broad daylight. A former race-car driver, Kovačević had become a "wealthy importer," but his murder wasn't just another of the anonymous gangland hits to which the public had grown accustomed. Kovačević was a close friend and associate of Milošević's son, Marko. They met while they were both involved in racing, and later went into business together. Their most profitable venture was a series of duty-free shops at border crossings, where their monthly turnover hovered between U.S. $3.5 and $4 million. Marko brought to the partnership his connection to the authorities, Kovačević's wife, Bojana, managed the business, and Kovačević, now a very well-connected bully, luxuriated. Marko's success delighted his mother, and she repeatedly boasted to friends that he was an excellent businessman. When Kovačević was murdered, the Miloševićs were extremely upset. Marko went to Greece the day after the funeral, and his sister, Marija, moved in with her parents until they were over the shock.

In another incident on 11 April 1997 at 12:30 A.M., the deputy minister of the Serbian police, Radovan Stojičić, joined his nineteen-year-old son, Vojislav, and Miloš Kurdulija, a customs official, in Belgrade's Mama Mia café. Mama Mia's was a police hangout, and Stojičić was a frequent patron. His son had asked that he join him there, and he arrived as he usually did without his bodyguards and ready to relax. Failing to take a precaution that is second nature to people in his line of work, he sat with his back to the entrance. A tall, heavy-set man wearing a balaclava rushed in and, waving a Heckler & Koch pistol, ordered everyone, including several police officers, to lie down on the floor. He walked to Vojislav Stojičić's table, put the muzzle of his gun against Stojičić's head, and fired just as Stojičić began to rise in surrender. Stojičić collapsed in a pool of blood, and his son and Kurdulija fled into the kitchen.

Stojičić, a poor miner's son, had had an action-packed career. Having commanded elite units during an Albanian miners' strike in Kosovo and again in battle near Vukovar during the war in Croatia, he became Serbia's chief of security, deputy minister of police, and also the first major general of the Serbian police. He was at the height of his career when someone's paid assassin strode into Mama Mia's and murdered him in cold blood.

Milošević was immediately informed and was so upset he didn't sleep that night. Stojičić had been entirely devoted to him, and as one of the few people Milošević really trusted, had been in charge of his personal security. If Serbia's chief of security was so vulnerable, who in Serbia was safe? At Stojičić's funeral Milošević was visibly distressed, and the leadership and Serbia's wealthy elite became panic-stricken. They all hired bodyguards, and Mirjana Marković, not trusting the police and worried about her own safety and that of her family, announced in one of her columns that a friend had warned her she would end up like Salvador Allende.

Stojičić's murder was taken as an indication that the regime would soon be overthrown. The police, having failed to protect their chief while he was alive, were reduced to dispatching units to his grave. But though graffiti alluding to Stojičić's murder announced, "I don't know what you've done, but I do know you deserved it," and many of the regime's individual victims cried for revenge, which neither the ubiquitous police nor the army and media could really prevent, no single Serbian organization was capable of toppling the regime. Still, there were fewer and fewer people the Miloševićs could trust. Even their closest allies, Dušan Mitević, for instance, an invaluable political strategist, and Bogoljub Karić, the wealthiest man in Serbia, were banished from their circle.

Bogoljub and his brothers, Sretan, Zoran, and Dragan, had amassed a vast fortune. Their parents, Kosovar Serbs who also had a daughter, had barely been able to keep them fed, and the brothers began to fend for themselves while they were still very young. But step by step they developed a business that began when Bogoljub, the youngest son, was sixteen. Although a mechanic by trade, he had demonstrated financial ability and convinced his brothers to set up shop in their home, manufacturing and selling hardware and minor farm implements. Bogoljub's enterprise and intelligence easily made up for his humble background and lack of education. His formula was that money is made "where the bourgeoisie won't tread," and in the late 1980s and early 1990s his family's business expanded throughout Serbia and into the former Soviet Union, two places in turmoil where business wasn't conducted with particular attention to formalities.

Bogoljub Karić's friendship with the Miloševićs began when the Union of Communists–Movement for Yugoslavia (CP-MY) was trying to sell part of the former Communist Party headquarters. Dušan Mitević introduced him to Mirjana Marković, who was also involved in the negotiations, and Karić, noticing that Tito's portrait hung in her office, complimented her for sticking to her beliefs. He and the Miloševićs were soon going on holidays and celebrating each other's patron saints' days together, and of course didn't fail to do each other favours, as is usual between friends. Milošević even persuaded Karić to buy the German ambassador's abandoned residence, located next door to his villa, so that they could all be closer.

The Karićs carefully planned everything in advance, including their children's future. For instance, rather than give birth in London where she lived, one of the Karić wives travelled to New York so that her child would be entitled to U.S. citizenship. The family then organized a cocktail party to celebrate the birth of Janičije II John Karić, a "future president of the United States of America." Two of Karić's nephews lived in Canada. One was a member of the Liberal Party, the other a Tory, so that no matter who was in power, the Karićs' Canadian business interests were protected. In Serbia, following the principle that one must respect and support governments but never so much as to anger those who might eventually replace them, Karić was on good terms with Šešelj, contributed to his party, and maintained contacts with other members of the opposition. And according to his wife, all of the Karićs voted against the Socialists in the early 1990s.

Karić's primary interest was business, but business and politics go hand in hand. Once he had amassed his fortune, he also wanted prestige, which in Serbia was to be found in government.

Milošević was aware of Karić's political ambitions and wanted to help. Demonstrating the full extent of his disregard for the political process, Milošević, who hired and fired officials as he saw fit and felt that only he could decide when he would step down, suddenly told Karić it was time to think about whom he was going to "leave Serbia to," and suggested that Karić take over the presidency. Anyone else would have been flabbergasted, but Karić simply took it for granted: "I can," he replied, "but only in 2005."

"Why only then?" enquired Milošević.

"Because I'll be turning fifty then, and I'll want to consolidate my business empire."

"That's too far off, Bogi, much too far off. I can't wait that long, I'm tired," Milošević replied in a tone indicating he was saddened by Karić's reticence. However, he enjoyed toying with Karić and had cast him some bait.

Inevitably Karić's relationship with the Miloševićs became complicated. Marković used Karić's jet on her travels abroad, and her holidays in Crete and countless other "favours" were paid for by him. For instance, Marija Milošević's Belgrade apartment was renovated at Karić's expense, and he financed a radio-television concern which she managed and partially owned. Marko Milošević, who had always hated school, obtained a diploma from Karić's university. Karić also financed close to twenty translated editions of Marković's books, and upon his intervention, she became a member of the Russian Academy of Arts and Sciences. He even arranged for her to meet with Patriarch Pavle, which so concerned Serbia's bishops that they anxiously called a meeting to discuss the situation. On the other hand, Karić's friendship with the Miloševićs was hardly unprofitable. While the Karićs had no trouble securing minor contracts on their own, major contracts were obtained through government intervention – as is the case in more developed countries, but especially so in Serbia, where one individual controls everything.

In early 1997 during the demonstrations many people were convinced that the regime was about to collapse, and Karić felt the time had come for him to enter politics. He frequently met with Šešelj and Drašković, was in touch with Vojvodinian students, and worked closely with Panić and Mitević. He readily acknowledged that he got what he paid for, and was in general a frank individual, even with the Miloševićs. But on one occasion he was rather too frank. He and the Miloševićs were discussing the Serbian government's incompetence and the possibility of replacing Mirko Marjanović, the president of Serbia's government. Karić offered to take over Marjanović's office if it were understood that he would then campaign for the presidency, since Milošević was "constitutionally limited to two terms in that office."

Karić had made two fatal errors: he had openly shown an interest in the leadership, and he had dared to suggest that Milošević wasn't entitled to a third term in office. In similar situations Milošević could react unpleasantly, but more often than not he remained detached. According to Karić, he graciously invited him to discuss the matter over lunch but didn't specify a date. Karić was satisfied – until more than a week later, when he realized that his lunch with Milošević would never materialize.

Karić's interest in politics wasn't motivated by potential financial rewards but rather by his desire for prestige and also the opportunity he would have to serve his nation. Having gathered enough support, he enthusiastically campaigned for the presidency, confident that the astrologer he had visited while in India with Marković wasn't mistaken when he had told him that all of his endeavours would succeed.

But Marković of course sided with her husband, and despite Karić's many favours, their friendship was over. The Miloševićs didn't comment on their new-found disapproval of Karić in public, nor did they need to. Upon little more than a nod, the press, having once portrayed Karić as a Serbian hero, embarked on a vicious campaign against him. The regime closed down his television station and challenged his ownership of the villa he had purchased in order to be closer to the Miloševićs. Coming to the belated conclusion that he had overstepped his bounds, and humiliated and frightened, Karić withdrew his candidacy. His business interests were being threatened, his political prospects were doubtful, and he had no choice but to protect his existing interests. Still, it was sad to see a man of such enormous wealth accept humiliation to appease the Miloševićs. His TV station became a propaganda outlet for the regime, and though he controlled most of Serbia's industrial output, he eventually took a post as one of the government's many junior ministers.

During YUL's first congress Karić congratulated Marković, saying that she and her party represented Serbia's future. She and Milošević eventually forgave him, and he, a man whose primary interests were commercial, accepted their forgiveness. His businesses hadn't been doing as well and required more capital, but he and his brothers never gave up and managed a turnaround. Their empire was safe, and that's what counted most.

Dušan Mitević also fell out of favour with the Miloševićs during this period. Mitević had been one of the first young communists to become a member of Serbia's leadership without having fought with the partisans. His political career began in the early 1960s when he was president of Serbia's Communist Youth League, and many people thought he would eventually become Serbia's president. However, he suddenly chose to abandon politics and went to work for RTB. Beginning as a trainee, he quickly became one of Serbia's leading journalists.

Although Mitević was deeply involved in Milošević's takeover during the 8th Plenary Session, and Milošević enjoyed his company and valued his advice, Milošević never fully trusted him and accepted his resignation in order to safeguard his hold on the leadership. But less than a year later everyone was begging for Mitević's return, and Marković, to whom Mitević was closer, brought him back in. As time passed, however, the ties between the Miloševićs and Mitević weakened. Mitević knew that Serbia was heading towards ruin and distanced himself, and Milošević wasn't reconciled to the fact that Mitević advised Panić and sat on the board of his Serbian joint venture.

Wishing to straighten Mitević out, Marković called a meeting during which she addressed him as though she were presiding over a Communist Party interrogation. "Duško," she said, "we're talking about you here, about your recent and overall behaviour." She then lectured him for half an hour, and enumerating his sins, accused him of protecting Karić and Panić and having defected to the opposition. "And you know what that means," she intoned. "You lied to us, you're working directly against the left, against our country."

When an earlier edition of this book appeared, the Miloševićs had been shocked to find their private lives had been exposed and that behind-the-scenes information, including secret conversations with their closest associates, had been divulged. They suspected Mitević, because, according to Marković, no one else knew that her bedroom was two steps away from Milošević's study.

Violent demonstrations were threatening to topple the regime, Stojičić and Marko Milošević's associate had recently been murdered, and the Miloševics suspected that there were plotters and spies in their midst. Now the usually soft-spoken Marković was banging her fists on the table, repeating the words "treason" and "vendetta" and telling Mitević that she and her family would hang if Milošević lost the upcoming election. At 9:00 P.M., she announced that anyone who wished to leave was free to go, and told Mitević she wouldn't do anything to harm him. "We need you, Duško," she insisted. Mitević arose, followed by Marković, and they shook hands and embraced. "Well, goodbye, Duško," she said, and began to cry.

Mitević patted her on the shoulder, turned to the others, and said, "Gentlemen, until we meet again." What he meant by "until we meet again" no one knew for sure, but Mitević's friendship with the Miloševics was over. Two years later, the government nationalized Panić's joint venture, and police, calling Mitević a "corrupt traitor" and a "western lackey," threw him out of his office.

The only one Marković could depend on now was Zoran Todorović, the owner of Beopetrol. Todorović, a vigorous thirty-eight-year-old father of two, was extremely dynamic, and many people, not imagining what the future would bring, thought he and his old friend Marković would continue to share many bright moments. However, on 24 October 1997, at about 8:00 A.M., Todorović pulled up to his headquarters in his black Mercedes and stopped before entering the building to exchange a few words with an acquaintance. A man who had appeared to be passing by drew an automatic weapon and fired. Todorović lay dead in a pool of blood, his acquaintance was severely wounded, and the assassin trotted off.

During the 1990s in Serbia the only path to wealth was to combine business with politics. Todorović, a political scientist by training, was from a working-class family. Motivated by a desire to escape the poverty he had known as a child, he went into politics as soon as he graduated from university, upon which his longstanding friendship with Marković enabled him to rise to the very heights of the Serbian establishment. Virtually overnight he became one of the richest men in Serbia, and second only to Marković, the most influential member of YUL's leadership. He was thus effectively the third most powerful individual in Serbia and was known among friends to have contemplated going after the presidency. While most people thought his murder was a gangland hit, his friends and colleagues at YUL were convinced that it was politically motivated.

Todorović was closer to Marković than anyone but Milošević. She tolerated his criticisms of her, and she criticized him even less than she criticized Milošević. Anything Todorović wanted was fine by Marković, and poems dedicated to her were found among his personal effects. Marković was in India at the time, promoting a textbook she had written. Only a death in her family could have affected her as much as Todorović's murder, and her associates argued amongst themselves to avoid having to break the news to her. When she was finally told, she at first tearfully denied what she had heard, and then, having sent her condolences through the Yugoslav embassy in New Dehi, isolated herself in her hotel room for thirty-six hours.

When Ljubiša Ristić read Marković's condolences at the funeral, Milošević wept. Though it was the first time he was seen to cry in public, his tears somehow failed to match his feelings for Todorović. It was known that he thought Todorović was annoyingly glib and insolent and only tolerated him out of devotion to his wife, whom he accompanied to Todorović's grave upon her return from India.

Although their ranks had been depleted, the Socialists and YUL remained in control of Serbia's government. The Miloševićs' closest allies were now Dragan Tomić, the president of Serbia's parliament, and Mirko Marjanović, the president of Serbia's government, both veterans of the regime whose talents for serving their master were unsurpassed.

18

All Roads Lead Away from Belgrade

The agenda dictated by the Americans at the Dayton conference needed to be implemented, meaning there was a price to pay for the war in Bosnia. Deciding who was to be held responsible wasn't a problem as everyone blamed the Serbs, but since Milošević had managed to avoid assuming personal responsibility by turning against the Pale leadership, they were held accountable and portrayed as bloodthirsty psychopaths – "criminals," in the words of Bill Richardson, America's ambassador to the United Nations. And with criminals the appropriate stance was clear.

Karadžić became a pariah well before Dayton. He was indicted for war crimes, excluded from negotiations, and forced to step down from the leadership of his party. Compromising him and forcing him to withdraw from public life was one of the Dayton conference's strategic objectives and was intended to weaken and demoralize the Bosnian Serbs.

In 1996 it was said that Karadžić had left Pale, and various press reports indicated that he had fled to Russia, Greece, Hilandar, or Chechnia. In fact he remained in Bosnia, living in a cottage he had built during the 1980s which he only left in utmost secrecy when there were important meetings to attend, so as to evade capture. He avoided talking about his future, but his friends said that he gave the impression of being a man who expected no mercy and who would rather have died than surrendered "like a coward."

His closest relatives supported him, and despite all the propaganda and legal pressures he faced, Karadžić, Bosnia's "most wanted criminal," not only remained popular among Bosnia's suffering and impoverished Serbs but indeed became a legend. He stood for their aspirations towards independent statehood, and was, as his fanatic followers affirmed, a "hidden source of light."

In contrast to Karadžić, General Ratko Mladić carried on as though he hadn't been indicted. Although he lost his military and political clout, his popularity was bolstered when, having suffered two strokes, he continued to circulate freely, attending the Belgrade funeral of his friend and fellow indictee General Djordje Djukić, and welcoming three hundred guests to his son's wedding in Belgrade's luxurious Hotel Intercontinental.

Throughout most of Serbia the indictments were taken as an indictment of the entire nation, and about a hundred Belgrade intellectuals, academicians, authors, and artists joined Patriarch Pavle in signing a petition calling for the indictments against Karadžić and Mladić to be dropped, arguing they had merely carried out their "legitimate democratic duties, according to the will of the people." Milošević was bound to cooperate with the international community, but concerns for his own security rather than any broader effect on his popularity prevented him from enforcing international arrest warrants against Karadžić and Mladić; both were capable of incriminating him.

Having reached an agreement in Dayton, Milošević could have chosen to sit back and leave the Bosnian leaders to their own devices, but as influence over them provided him with leverage within the international community, he remained involved. With Karadžić now barred from assuming an official role, Milošević was able to divide the Bosnian leadership, which he had failed to do during the war.

When the Bosnian Serbs' Republic of Srpska became legitimate, its leadership immediately quarrelled over which city would become its capital: Pale or Banja Luka. Eventually the entire population and all of their institutions were torn over the issue, and the new republic separated into western and eastern halves, the former led by Dr Biljana Plavšić and the latter by Momčilo Krajišnik. There were no contacts between them, and the rift was accepted by their constituents. The factions became so bitterly opposed that without the presence of UN peacekeepers the fragile new republic would have been overrun by Bosnia's Muslims and Croats.

Claiming that he was arbitrating between them to ensure that Dayton's terms were being respected, Milošević attempted to remove the wartime leadership and install his allies. He especially abhorred Plavšić, who frequently denounced the Miloševićs. According to her, Milošević was a traitor who had brought suffering and humiliation upon the Serbs. She challenged him to abandon communism and ask for Serb forgiveness, and she denounced Marković as a "wicked, deceitful, and manipulative power-monger."

Meanwhile there was no news from Karadžić. He and his bodyguards had left Pale, and his family didn't know where he was hiding. His wife, who worked as a psychiatrist in Pale's sanitarium, told reporters that even his friends were having trouble getting in touch with him. But the West, with more urgent matters to attend to in the Balkans, no longer seemed interested in his capture.

Having failed to remove the wartime leadership, Milošević sought a temporary ally in Krajišnik, Karadžić's second-in-command, who was more flexible than his peers. But Plavšić and Milorad Dodik were supported by the Americans and of course won their struggle against Krajišnik. Dodik had been a capable entrepreneur and became a politician who understood that the only solution was to submit to the West. After six long years there seemed to be hope for the Bosnian Serbs. Plavšić and Krajišnik lost their electoral bid for the leadership in 1997, but Carlos Vestendorp, the EU high commissioner for Bosnia and Hercegovina, was really in charge, and Milošević was out of the picture.

Wherever Milošević failed to unilaterally impose his political will and install his allies, there were dire consequences – even in his ancestral homeland of Montenegro, where such problems were least expected. The Montenegrin leadership had risen to power in 1989 on a wave of popular enthusiasm for the notion that Serbia and Montenegro were a large family. The former Communist leaders were ousted, and Momir Bulatović, Milo Djukanović, and Svetozar Marović, three highly educated and capable young men, replaced them, in an effusion of warmth and solidarity among Serbs and Montenegrins.

However, once the war in Bosnia was lost, the Montenegrins became less and less accepting of their republic's subordinate role in Yugoslavia and of the isolation they endured as a result of their union with Serbia. Initially the leadership avoided conflict and attempted to strike a balance between its party-based loyalty to Milošević and independence from Serbia. By supporting Milošević, they remained secure within the ruling party, and by demonstrating their unease regarding the state of affairs in Serbia, they were granted economic advantages for Montenegro by the international community that increased their popular support.

Shortly before Dayton, Marković had overstepped what the Montenegrins felt were acceptable bounds of their union with Serbia and engaged her party in an attempt to challenge their leadership. Prime Minister Djukanović announced that YUL, representing "abstract, retrograde ideals," had no place in Montenegro. Marković countered by stating that Djukanović was a "Johnny-Come-Lately Montenegrin separatist" whose political office was merely a "front for his smuggling operation." Milošević stood by her, though at the time his hold on the leadership was precarious; anyone who was aware of the full extent of her influence knew that Djukanović was in trouble.

Milošević resorted to proven tactics, and Montenegro was soon divided. Djukanović's camp included the church, and Milošević's camp, which included Montenegro's poor, was represented by Momir Bulatović. Though Bulatović had sided with the international community and advocated Montenegrin independence during former Yugoslavia's breakup, his great advantage was that he had not used his office to amass a personal fortune. But a politician's true nature only becomes apparent under pressure, and Bulatović soon became Belgrade's main supporter in Montenegro.

On the eve of presidential elections in Montenegro Milošević sent a group of leading Serbian officials to Podgorica, formerly Titograd, to rally support for Bulatović. They expected an enthusiastic reception, but instead their vehicles were swarmed by thousands of demonstrators and pelted with produce and rocks. Had it not been for the police, Dragan Tomić, the president of Serbia's parliament, would have been dragged out of his car and certainly beaten.

Montenegro had traditionally been divided regarding its union with Serbia, but pro-Yugoslavs were in the majority. Djukanović was sensitive to the issue and formed an alliance with the Serbian opposition, stressing that he was opposed to the Miloševićs' "fascist regime" but not to Montenegro's union with Serbia. He narrowly defeated Bulatović, upon which Bulatović and Belgrade accused him of fraud. Thousands of Bulatović's followers, many of them armed, took to the streets, parading Lenin's portrait and Communist flags. Eighty-three police and eleven demonstrators were injured when a grenade was thrown among police who were preventing the demonstrators from storming parliament. Civil war seemed imminent.

Djukanović compromised by abandoning his alliance with the Serbian opposition, but Milošević, whom he called a "political dinosaur," didn't congratulate him on his victory, didn't schedule meetings of the federal government for seven months, and appointed Bulatović prime minister of Yugoslavia, an office Djukanović called the "Montenegrin government in exile." Nevertheless, Djukanović remained convinced that Montenegro needed to remain in Yugoslavia. He announced in his inaugural address, "Throughout history, Serbia and the Serbian people have never had a more sincere and devoted friend than Montenegro. That's the way it's always been, and that's how it will remain during my term in office." Though many people were disappointed that he hadn't taken a more courageous stand, he continued to oppose Milošević's regime. His government opened independent missions abroad, established its own currency, and refused to get involved in the emerging crisis in Kosovo.

Once again Yugoslavia had become a fictitious entity. Though Milošević's disastrous policies had helped Slovenia and Croatia achieve independence, most Montenegrins were initially happy to remain in Yugoslavia. But as Yugoslavia became a pariah, they began to question the union and quietly embarked on a once unfathomable but now inevitable path.

Similarly, the Republic of Srpska had long been under Belgrade's dominion, and the Bosnian Serbs only began their difficult affirmation of their own political identity once they became free of Milošević. Where this would lead them remained to be seen, but at least they understood that nothing positive could be expected from any alliance with Milošević's regime.

19

Serbian Blunders in Kosovo

The Yugoslav crisis, which began in Kosovo, came full circle ten years later in January 1999 when NATO's commander, General Wesley Clarke, presented Milošević with an ultimatum: Serbia would be bombarded if its troops didn't pull out of the province. Milošević thought he was bluffing, and replied that he would rather die than yield Kosovo.

Kosovo is the cradle of Serbian civilization, a place where the nation's origins and spiritual roots are preserved. But though Serbs regard Kosovo as their holy land, they still managed to lose hold of it. Their struggles against the Albanian Kosovars were counter-productive, and the Albanians had had a strategy in place for creating a greater Albanian state since the late 1960s. Ultimately they won their greatest victory against their greatest foe, Slobodan Milošević.

A decade-long illusory peace was achieved in Kosovo by rescinding the province's autonomy, which bolstered Milošević's regime. But the Albanian Kosovars were in no hurry, and more importantly, they were united. Within a state they refused to recognize, they maintained a parallel government that included their own president, parliament, diplomacy, health care, education, and economy, as well as an independent press that openly advocated separatism. And though the prisons of the Milošević regime were full of activists who would become the core of the Kosovo Liberation Army (KLA), Albanian Kosovar political leaders weren't harassed.

In 1988 Milošević had brutally ousted an entire generation of moderate Albanian leaders, who had made it possible to hold at bay the bloodier disputes between Serbs and Albanians. These leaders were replaced by separatists led by Ibrahim Rugova, who appeared on the political scene in the 1990s and was more flexible than his peers.

Rugova had shown an interest in politics while he was a student, but he wasn't a revolutionary. Seemingly fragile, taciturn, and unprepossessing, he wears glasses and often wraps himself in a shawl, an appearance that tends to suggest that he is someone who would choose a more sedate occupation than politics. Though he participated in the Kosovar Albanian student revolts of 1968, he was still a member of the Communist Party and didn't belong to the student leadership. Neither was he among the extremists in the 1981 revolts in the province. During that time, while a crisis raged in cities throughout Kosovo, Rugova, a respected critic, essayist, and translator from the French, sat at home preparing a study of Pjeter Bogdanij, a seventeenth-century founder of Albanian literature. But subsequently his politics brought him to oppose Milošević, and just as Milošević's policies helped Tudjman, Kućan, and Izetbegović, he also made possible the ascent of Rugova and other Kosovars.

After Dayton, Milošević's international standing improved, and he could easily have made a deal with the Albanian leaders by extending an olive branch and offering their province a greater degree of autonomy. But Milošević never sought political solutions and always lagged behind the curve, obsessed with petty manoeuvres to ensure that he remained in power. He addressed burning issues once they could no longer be resolved or resolved them at the Serbian people's expense. He thought his followers and the Serbian police would keep him in power forever, and Rugova's boycott of Serbian elections, which brought him an additional thirty seats in parliament, was convenient. Though the Albanian separatists and Milošević's Socialists were bitter enemies, they served each other well. The Albanians' boycott gave the Socialists a majority in parliament, and by ignoring 800,000 Kosovar voters, the Socialists gave the Albanians additional proof that their situation in Kosovo was untenable. But the situation the

Kosovar Serbs were in was no better, because all of the province's resources, both political and financial, were in the hands of a small privileged minority of Milošević's followers.

A violent outcome seemed inevitable. Serbs couldn't imagine their nation without its southern province, and the Albanians could no longer fathom living with the Serbs. People on both sides proclaimed that they would rather die than give up Kosovo, and though Serbs continued to move out of the province, international opinion was bombarded with the Albanians' complaints and accusations. Serbian Kosovo was a "prison" from which they wanted freedom, and as Serbs were widely perceived as the scourge responsible for Yugoslavia's violent breakdown, Rugova's cause was embraced in the West. He not only met with Bill Clinton but also received humanitarian awards from France, the Czech Republic, and the European Community.

The Albanian uprising began when peaceful demonstrations were held in Kosovo's larger cities, but it escalated into a surprisingly powerful armed insurrection during the spring of 1998. The KLA had assembled thirty thousand fanatics and mercenaries and was receiving arms shipments from many nations – Albania in particular, which provided the insurgents with a million Kalashnikov assault rifles. Mercenaries arrived from Germany, Slovenia, and Croatia, and the rebels were trained by American, British, and German instructors.

Life in Kosovo became extremely difficult for anyone who didn't support the KLA, including Albanians who opposed armed insurrection. Within five months the KLA had killed thirty-three border guards and wounded ninety-six others. Sixty-two Serbian police were killed and 197 wounded, and 262 non-Albanians were being held in prison camps. Serbia then engaged its troops, and a real war broke out during which there were many victims on both sides, and columns of refugees abandoned their homes in search of safety. Both sides were guilty of crimes, and the number of innocents who died will never be known, but the western media only reported on the ethnic cleansing of Albanians, which was compared to Cambodia's killing fields.

The Americans' objective was to land troops in Kosovo, which Milošević, fearing the threat they would represent to his regime, refused to accept. In order to convince the international community that Serbia would "defend Kosovo to the last man," a referendum was organized on the basis of the leading question: Would the citizens of Serbia accept foreign intervention in Kosovo? Thanks to the Serbian media and electoral fraud, Milošević always got what he wanted, and the referendum was no exception. Serbia was bombarded with seemingly patriotic slogans designed to confirm his agenda, and over five million Serbs, or 95 per cent of the population, supported him.

Milošević hoped the referendum would give him leverage against the Americans, but then for the first time in ten years he bowed to their pressure and agreed to meet with the Albanian leadership. He cordially greeted Ibrahim Rugova and his associates, accompanied by a police escort, at the White Palace. Among them was Mahmut Bakali, a former president of the Communist Party of Kosovo who had been banned from politics following the 1981 Kosovo uprising. As Bakali had frequently visited the White Palace during his days in the leadership, Milošević made him feel welcome by cheerfully suggesting that he was better acquainted with the White Palace than Milošević was himself. He was similarly personable with the entire delegation and had apparently been well briefed on each of its members. But when he told Veton Suroji, a publisher, that the government had no concerns over his newpapers, Suroji replied that they had been shut down.

"No way," replied Milošević. "When?" Suroji anwered Milošević, adding that the problem he wished to address wasn't whether this or that paper had been banned but other things Milošević's government was responsible for, such as the massacre of Albanian civilians in Prekaz.

The talks, which lasted only from noon until 1:30 P.M., focused on an agreement that would have provided for a negotiated solution to the conflict. But instead of staying for lunch with their host, the Albanians went to the residence of American Ambassador Richard Miles, where their fate was actually being determined. No further talks took place between Milošević and the Albanians, perhaps because there had not been enough bloodshed to warrant them, and the war in Kosovo only intensified.

Although the Serbian opposition, or what remained of it, was no longer a threat, the situation in Kosovo presented the regime with an excellent opportunity to co-opt it members. Šešelj's never-ending threats and provocations made Milošević look like a wise and dignified statesman. Drašković came back to life, supporting the referendum and calling for a state of emergency. He urged the government to send more troops into Kosovo, to go to the "Serbian holy land" and seek out Albanians behind "each and every bush." He even visited Kosovo himself, where, only encouraging the Serbian police, he asked where more Albanian terrorists could be found. As a reward Drašković was given control of Belgrade's municipal government. This included the highly influential Studio B television station which he turned into his own propaganda outlet, quickly dismissed by his opponents as "Vukovision."

Milošević could rest easy. Šešelj and Drašković had become devoted supporters of the regime and continued to antagonize each other. A leaflet circulated by the student organization Otpor summed up the situation: "Idiots, representing idiots, creating yet more idiots, are in control of this country."

During the autumn of 1998 the war in Kosovo turned to the Serbs' advantage. Their troops had destroyed the rebels' primary units, but NATO, still bent on sending troops to the province, announced that it would intervene in order to prevent a humanitarian catastrophe. Jets were on standby, "all of Europe" supported NATO, and Serbia's neighbours, Croatia, Hungary, Rumania, Albania, and Macedonia, offered their assistance.

But in Serbia, where graffiti mocked the alliance, NATO's threats still weren't taken seriously. Milošević remained convinced that the West's representatives were bluffing, and his wife engaged in pathetic attempts to rally the nation, suggesting that if Yugoslavia caved in to the ultimatum, small nations' hopes for freedom and justice would collapse, and the world's progress towards a better future would be dealt a severe blow.

Milošević and Richard Holbrooke, both aggressive and vain masters of brinkmanship, talked for days on end. When Holbrooke introduced Milošević to NATO air commander General Michael Short, the first thing Milošević said was, "So, general, you're the man who's going to bomb us!" The general, both full of himself and eager for a war that would serve to justify his rank, memorably replied that he had "B52s in one hand, U2s in the other." As a result of their talks, Milošević accepted two thousand European observers being sent to Kosovo.

The referendum was no longer mentioned, but Milošević's acceptance of foreign observers failed to dampen his support. Having been praised for refusing intervention, he was now praised for accepting it. His supporters announced that they admired his leadership during the negotiations, as well as his "superhuman endurance," and suggested that he would go down in history as "the man who averted World War III." Thus, a resounding "NO" to foreign intervention yielded to an equally resounding "YES," and NATO easily took control of Kosovo.

The international community backed off, and the threat of bombardment seemed to have been defused. Milošević could now focus on problems within Serbia, which included dissension from the remaining independent media, Belgrade University, and a few disloyal officials. Though the regime was in control of the mass media, a few small outlets continued to trouble Milošević. He and his government had spent many years taming the independent press and still considered it a serious threat. In the midst of the Kosovo crisis, the *Daily Telegraph*, *Today*, and *Our Struggle* were banned for instilling "fear, panic, and defeatism" into the population, and "negatively impacting citizens' willingness to protect Yugoslavia's sovereignty and territorial integrity."

Milošević had a "patriotic" new law enacted that enforced a complete ban on all independent media. Subversive members of the press weren't merely threatened with arrest or closure but were fined so heavily they either censured themselves or were forced out of business. It was by far the most contemptible and repressive law ever to burden the media. At a time when monthly wages averaged 1,125 dinars, the fines were in excess of two million dinars. While owners of independent media quickly transferred their property to their families, propaganda suggested that the new law was in fact a "great legacy for European civilization."

The ultimate price was eventually paid by Slavko Čuruvija, an oustanding journalist who owned the *Daily Telegraph* and *The European*. In the midst of NATO raids on Serbia on Easter Sunday, 11 April 1999, Čuruvija went for an afternoon walk. On his way home he passed a pair of youths dressed in black, and moments later sixteen rounds were fired into his back. Branka Prpa, who

witnessed the murder, told me the assassins finished him off with
two rounds to the head. Čuruvija was an extraordinarily courageous, strong willed, and adventuresome human being, and his
death was a tremendous loss. His assassins were never caught,
but rumours, which inevitably surround unsolved murders,
suggested that he was killed for defaulting on debt he had in-
curred following the regime's seizure of his papers. In any case, as
he had systematically opposed the regime, it was highly likely that
his murder was political. When Prpa asked the detective in charge
of the case whether there were any suspects, he was told that
"ordinary criminals never commit murder on Easter."

Čuruvija's assassination is a poignant example of just how
difficult it was to be a journalist in Serbia. He had refused to
abandon his wry polemic against the regime and thus assumed
certain obvious risks. But though he exposed government corruption, he knew that the sword he wielded was double-edged and
had therefore sought protection within the regime, as was usual
among even the most independent of journalists. Čuruvija's
patron within the regime was Mirjana Marković.

Čuruvija and Marković became friends when they discovered
their shared nostalgia for the former Yugoslavia. Marković, while
charmed by his wit and openness, also appreciated the fact that he
was the owner of two influential newspapers. Čuruvija was of
course aware of the influence Milošević wielded in government
and once told me that freedom abounded in his papers – except
where Marković and her children were concerned. He hardly
knew how fine a line he was walking, and how unproductive it
was to polemicize the regime without inside approval. When the
law that destroyed the independent media was enacted, he decided he would no longer refrain from criticizing the Miloševićs.
He told Marković that Serbia was becoming a fascist state and that
bloodshed was no more than six or seven months away. Marković
flew into a rage and denounced him as a foreign spy.

Two months before he was murdered, Čuruvija had been in
Washington, and told u.s. congressmen that since Milošević had
put him out of business, his only option was to do everything he
could to bring down the regime. Many others felt the same way
and were also hounded out of business.

The regime was extremely wary of the opposition that Belgrade University was capable of harnessing. Its students were always the most belligerent participants in any demonstration, and its faculty was highly respected throughout Serbia. The regime then enacted another law effectively giving it control of the university. The rectorate, deanships, and faculty appointments were now determined by party affiliation, and Belgrade University was taken over by members of YUL, the Socialist Party, and even a few Radicals.

Simultaneously Milošević ousted the army chief of staff and the chief of the Secret Police. Although General Momčilo Perišić, the chief of staff, was a disciplined soldier, he was hardly a puppet and was therefore considered too independent to remain at his post. He had met with and supported students during the demonstrations in 1996 and 1997, and not wishing to involve the JNA in a political struggle, he kept silent during the conflict between Djukanović and Bulatović in Montenegro. Also, he blamed Yugoslavia's isolation and the war in Kosovo on the leadership: "If everyone had done their job," he said, "it wouldn't have come to this."

Although his fellow officers respected Perišić's military virtues and lack of pretence, Milošević felt he couldn't be trusted. For instance, during a meeting on Kosovo, Milan Milutinović took Richard Holbrook aside and told him that "the Chief" preferred not to discuss certain issues in front of Perišić. Upon his dismissal, Perišić announced that the government had "no use for men of integrity and independent spirit" and added that while he had been discharged "without discussion, without precedent, and illegally," he remained at the disposition of "the army, the nation, and its people."

Marković was of course involved in these purges. According to Ćuruvija, she told her associates that Perišic and another ousted official, Jovica Stanišić, Serbia's chief of security, had planned to stage a coup.

Milošević then took care of the opposition. Šešelj was already Serbia's deputy prime minister, and Drašković, who no longer collaborated with the other members of the opposition, accepted Milošević's offer to join his government. He became Yugoslavia's vice president, and his party obtained a few ministerial portfolios.

The independent press had been eradicated, Belgrade University was taken over, and the opposition had been co-opted. Only a very few underground organizations still opposed the regime and expressed the bitterness felt by many Serbs – the student group Otpor, for instance, whose emblem, a clenched fist, spoke eloquently of the only option that was still open to Serbs: forceful resistance.

However, our concerns about Miloševič, his regime, and the useless opposition soon paled in comparison to our next problem, which had us all asking whether we'd live to see another day.

20

Gods of War

Milošević believed that the foreign observers he had allowed into Kosovo would prevent NATO from carrying out its threats. But as far as the Americans were concerned, the observers represented the initial phase of an occupation of Kosovo which they hoped would be sanctioned by an agreement between Serbia and the Kosovar Albanians. In February their delegations met inconclusively in Rambouillet, France, and then towards the middle of March gathered again in Paris. Nothing was achieved at either conference, first of all because Serbia's position on the matter was a question of national pride, and secondly, because the West attempted to force its will upon the Serbs.

Belgrade was asked to withdraw its troops so that an international protectorate could be established. Yugoslavia's sovereignty was to be guaranteed, but the agreement was to stipulate that the final outcome would be determined democratically, through elections to be held within three years. Given that at least 90 per cent of Kosovo's population was Albanian, the Serbs doubted the assurances they were given regarding their sovereignty. In fact the agreement was an ultimatum, and Madeleine Albright imperiously announced that unless the Serbs accepted, they would be bombarded. Similar crises had arisen throughout the globe, in Cyprus and the Middle East, Northern Ireland, Burma, Azerbaijan, Turkey, and Mexico, but no such threat had ever been made before.

Furthermore, the Serbs were humiliated by the Americans' decision to exclude Ibrahim Rugova and other moderate Albanians from the talks in favour of the vicious and fanatical KLA. Rugova sat in the third row, a mere observer, while the Albanian delegation was led by Hasim Tači, the KLA's political leader. Tači, who held a degree in history, had graduated from a military academy in Albania's capital, Tirana. He had belonged to a terrorist organization with roots in the Albanian diaspora, and a Serbian court had sentenced him in absentia to ten years in prison. And there he sat, nestled among his American advisors.

The talks fell through, but many Serbs felt they would resume, not imagining that a military orgy unlike anything Europe had witnessed in over fifty years was about to begin. As determined as the Americans were to meet their objectives through force, they still hoped Milošević would come to his senses. But Milošević, persisting in his belief that NATO was bluffing, felt that he could continue to play cat-and-mouse with the Americans and still reach an agreement. However, when the second round of talks fell through, he decided to face their threat and made himself clear on the matter when he and Richard Holbrooke met one last time in Belgrade:

"Do you realize what will happen if the talks fall through?"

"Yes, I do – you will bombard us!"

"Let me be clear. The operation will be intense, brutal, uncompromising."

"Your involvement is over; there will be no more negotiations, and you will bombard us."

On 22 March 1999 Serbia's parliament enacted a resolution according to which the presence of foreign troops in Kosovo was rejected, and two days later Radio B-92 informed listeners that NATO's military action against Serbia had been approved. On 26 March police erupted into its studios and took Veran Matić, B-92's director, to their headquarters for what was described as an "informative little talk." Saša Mirković, the station manager, was subsequently fired, and not too long after that Serbia's most influential independent radio station was shut down. A staff member then announced that "due to technical difficulties" B-92 would no longer be transmitting. According to Dragan Tomić, the president of Serbia's parliament, the station's transmitter would have facilitated NATO's targeting of Belgrade.

On 24 March at 5:00 A.M., U.S. Ambassador Richard Miles had left Belgrade for Budapest, taking 320 document-filled boxes with him. In the rush many foreign diplomats departed with little more then the clothes they were wearing, and nineteen Americans abandoned their possessions in Belgrade.

Church officials announced that they were praying for "peace, justice, safety, and freedom for everyone in Kosovo, Serbia, and throughout the globe, and for the wisdom of its secular leaders." But their prayers went unanswered. At 8:14 P.M., the first ghastly sirens were heard, and bombs began to fall on Serbia. During seventy-eight days of helpless terror and destruction, neither Serbia nor the international community, in which countless Serbs had placed their hopes, lived up to their expectations of each other. NATO's General Secretary Xavier Solana announced that the attack on Yugoslavia was "an attempt to defend the moral values" upon which Europe was entering the twenty-first century, and Joschka Fischer, the German minister of foreign affairs, stated that NATO was not attacking but rather resisting Serbian aggression. But there was in fact no risk involved for NATO. The outcome was clear, and NATO's forces and their Serbian enemies never met eye to eye, an unprecedented occurrence in the annals of war.

NATO's nineteen members, representing 600 million people, were supported by virtually all European nations. They attacked a small pariah, deploying their most advanced weaponry in order to destroy our nation from a safe distance. Bridges, highways, power lines, refineries, and Serbia's electrical grid were demolished, as were factories upon which hundreds of thousands of workers' livelihoods depended. Television studios, residential buildings, hospitals, passenger-laden buses and trains, and even the Chinese embassy were attacked. Within twenty days more Serbian property was destroyed than during the entire Second World War.

The West had tolerated Milošević as long as he was useful, and when he no longer was, Serbia's innocent citizens became its victims. Having been oppressed by Milošević's government, they were now fodder in a war that was primarily a testing-ground for NATO's might.

Most Americans didn't even know where Kosovo was, nor did their media, whose orchestrated reports echoed the campaign against Serbia. CNN, the most influential global news organization,

announced that a bridge crossing the Danube had been destroyed
in the capital of Vojvodina, Novi Sad, which it identified as "the
second largest city in Kosovo." And Christopher Hill, a highly
vocal Washington diplomat, obviously didn't take the time to read
up on the province's thousand-year history and announced that
the Serbs had taken Kosovo from the Albanians in 1912.

The attacks were justified as a way of preventing a humanitarian catastrophe. The U.S. State Department claimed that 500,000
Albanians were unaccounted for and were feared to have become
the "victims of genocide." The western media, which aired
striking images of the refugees, announced that between 800,000
and a million of them had been forced to flee the onslaught of
Serbia's troops. It was all designed to justify the West's aggression
and was far from the truth. Prior to the Albanians' armed insurrection, there were no large-scale relocations, and for thirty years
the Serbs' own prospects in Kosovo had been so grim that many of
them were in fact leaving the province. Albanians only began to
flee in large numbers when the war broke out, at which point they
became the victims of NATO war planes, their own extremist
compatriots, and Serbian paramilitaries. Innocent Kosovar Serbs
would pay dearly for the paramilitaries' crimes, many of which
remain concealed. Patriarch Pavle was the first to denounce these
acts and said that the "Serbian nation's soul is stained with
Albanian blood." However, both sides were guilty of atrocities,
and mass graves containing the remains of both Serbs and Albanians are still being uncovered.

Though both Serbs and Albanians were victims of the region's
insane politics, the tragedy was exclusively blamed on Serbs. The
Albanian leadership benefited from the Serbs' reputation in the
international community and incited Albanian Kosovars to flee
the province, knowing that their departure would provide a basis
for the West's attack on Serbia. However, no one mentioned that
100,000 citizens of Serbia fled from Kosovo during the war,
seeking shelter from the raids.

Officially NATO was conducting the raids, but the war was in
fact an American aggression against Serbia, and 80 per cent of the
aircraft involved were American. The British were also heavily
involved, and their youthful prime minister, Tony Blair, even
helped determine Serbian targets. The western media referred to

him, Madeleine Albright, and NATO's Wesley Clarke as the "gods of war."

Slovenia, Croatia, Bosnia, the Czech Republic, Slovakia, Hungary, Macedonia, and even tiny Lichtenstein offered logistical support, and Bulgaria, which had yielded its territory to the Third Reich in 1941 as a staging ground for the invasion of Yugoslavia, now yielded its airspace to NATO. Subsequently they all lined up, waiting for their exemplary behaviour to be rewarded by the Americans. A Sarajevan daily even compared Sonya Licht, the director of the Soros Foundation, to Šešelj for having dared denounce the bombing of Belgrade. Alija Izetbegović said that "NATO's attack on Yugoslavia needed to be carried out earlier," and was joined by the former president of Croatia's Communist Party, Ivica Račan, whose only comment was: "Finally!" And Agim Ceku – an Albanian former JNA officer who became a general in the Croatian Army, participated in the massacre of innocent Serbs, and was then decorated nine times by Croatia – became the KLA's commander.

Serbs were brought together by the raids, and despite the many hardships they faced, including wage shortages, no one complained about the regime. Once the initial psychological impact of the attacks was overcome, people went about their business as though nothing unusual were happening and even defiantly ignored air-raid warnings. Citizens at first gathered spontaneously, demonstrating their solidarity, but gradually as NATO attacks continued it became obvious that free concerts given by Serbian pop stars and similar events were being contrived by the regime.

Milošević had been Serbia's sovereign ruler for more than a decade, and his years in power marked Serbia's decline. Many Serbs came to despise the Miloševićs' regime, but NATO's raids served to redirect their mounting intolerance of the regime toward America, Great Britain, and France, traditional allies from whom democrats in Serbia expected assistance, not bombardment.

Serbian propaganda then announced a momentous event. Upon Šešelj's recommendation, Yugoslavia's parliament decided to seek an alliance with Russia and Belorus. Šešelj announced ecstatically that with the Russians on our side, no one could harm us, and Dragan Tomić, who specialized in justifying poor policy decisions with incoherent statements, said that a "gold rubric" would mark the historical event. However, as could be expected, a discouraging reply was soon heard. Russia was barely surviving and depended on the West; it would do anything for its brethren except provide them with modern weapons – or, heaven forbid, go to war against the Americans. "An alliance with Serbia must be approached reasonably, and with calm; it is something to consider for the future," Boris Yeltsin announced.

For Serbs, the NATO aircraft that they ironically called "guardian angels" came to symbolize the undeclared war. NATO's strategic objective was to destroy Serbia's military and industrial capacity and communications and turn the country into a desolate enclave. Roads and communications between Vojvodina and Serbia, Serbia and Montenegro, and many cities within Serbia were destroyed, and to travel, for instance, between Podgorica and Belgrade, one had to take a detour through Sarajevo. And that was just the beginning, for a civilian bloodbath ensued which NATO casually referred to as "operational mistakes," "collateral damage" – and even "linguistic confusion," which meant that NATO aviators had misread their maps.

Jamie Shea, an Oxford PhD, whose dissertation examined the role of the European intellectual after World War I, coldly announced that NATO was "honestly working toward peace." "However," he added, "mistakes are unavoidable," and NATO wouldn't be sidetracked. The mistakes he was referring to included four hundred families who lost everything they owned; a rocket attack on a train in which fourteen civilians died; twenty civilians dead, including nine children between the ages of five and twelve in a small town of nineteen thousand inhabitants; sixteen civilians dead when a rocket hit a bus; twenty more dead and forty wounded among refugees from Croatia and Bosnia who were sheltering in a hospital; and eleven dead and forty wounded on a bridge in Varvarina on the Feast of the Holy Trinity, including Miloje Čirić, a clergyman, who was decapitated by shrapnel.

In order to teach the Serbs a lesson, more helpless civilians died when RTB's studios were attacked. The patriotic director had forced his employees to keep working at night when the raids were usually carried out, and paid no attention to the fact that two days prior to the attack CNN staff had abandoned their nearby offices. On 23 April 1999 at 2:15 A.M., while the director was safely at home, the studios were hit by NATO rockets and sixteen young men and women died. During the victims' memorial service, their bereaved family and friends accused the director of murder and attacked his car as he was leaving.

NATO believed that Milošević would surrender soon after the first raids began, not expecting that Serbia, weakened by war, sanctions, and poverty, could endure such a tremendous assault. But the army was no longer the same institution that had stood helplessly by as former Yugoslavia collapsed; and though Milošević gave precedence to the police, the army demonstrated that it was extremely well organized and confounded the enemy with brilliant decoys. Overall, the government dealt with the raids far better than expected, but the highest recognition went to employees who maintained Yugoslavia's electrical grid. According to the western press, they were among the war's great heroes.

Milošević always found ways to manipulate public opinion. Having long considered the army incompetent, he suddenly declared that it was "invincible" and made frequent appearances among its generals. As the army was successfully defending the country, Milošević, its commander-in-chief, became a "symbol of struggle and resistance," whose leadership was exalted in a series of propagandistic telegrams from an adoring public, stating that he was the most "able and cunning commander in Serbian history."

Milošević was of course a target himself, but he moved about incessantly and availed himself of underground bunkers that had been built for Tito. His residence was hit during a rocket attack, but the incident was more a warning than an attempt to murder him, and he and Marković had ample time to take shelter.

Given the state of emergency, everything was under government control. The independent press had already been eradicated, but all media were subjected to censure during the raids. Still, no one complained, because there was only one enemy at the time: NATO. More than 50 per cent of the electorate had opposed the regime and looked to the West for support in their struggle for democracy, but when Serbia was attacked by nations whose flags they had admiringly carried during months of protest, towns governed by the opposition, ironically, suffered the heaviest damage.

The opposition became completely insignificant, and though its leaders all denounced the raids, the regime continued to pressure them, especially Djindjić, who received death threats and fled to Montenegro. He and Milo Djukanović were then labelled as vultures who were sabotaging the nation's defence.

The Church deeply regretted the death of civilians and denounced the regime. Patriarch Pavle insisted that there could be no positive outcome to the war against NATO and the Albanians, and wanted the regime to compromise. During one of his frequent meetings with Dobrica Ćosić, Ćosić told him that Serbia would be forced to surrender. "Don't call it a surrender," the patriarch replied. "Say that they will force us to relent. God gave man the capacity to choose between right and wrong, and also the ability to survive. It is life, and not death, that must determine our earthly existence. Our cause is just," the patriarch concluded, "but we must survive in order to defend it."

The raids went on for months. In all, NATO dropped five times more explosives on Serbia than had been used during the entire siege of Stalingrad. At first citizens endured their ordeal and were defiant, but as the raids continued and death became ever more present, defiance yielded to exhaustion and despair. Serbs just wanted the nightmare to end, no matter on what terms.

Though many young men expressed their support for their country by going about in uniform, the regime was clearly to blame, and no attempt to mobilize the nation would have succeeded. While the Serb poor in Kosovo suffered and died, the regime's members sheltered their families. President Milutinović's son went to study in England, and rather than enlist in the army, Marko Milošević strutted comfortably about Požarevac in combat fatigues, surrounded by bodyguards. However, it would be unfair to say that he didn't contribute to the war effort, for in the midst of the raids, he opened an amusement park.

In an attempt to suggest that there was massive support of the war effort in Kosovo, propaganda announced that Serbs were writing the "definitive text on patriotism." Yet despite propaganda and deflated casualty reports, many families refused to give up their sons. Officially, between the onset of the state of emergency and the withdrawal of Serbian troops from Kosovo, there were only about 650 casualties. During the same period, 4,300 men failed to appear for conscription, all of whom were indicted by the regime. Of these, 1,990 were contested and are currently being investigated.

Amid mounting concern anti-war protests were held in a number of Serbian cities, and reservists suggested that Marko Milošević enlist. In Kruševac 5,000 residents, primarily mothers, demanded that their sons, husbands, and fathers be returned alive.

Meanwhile the Serbian economy reverted to the condition it was in at the turn of the century. With the exception of a handful of profiteers, Serbs who were lucky enough to survive barely subsisted. Approximately 2,000 civilians were killed, and more than 6,000 were wounded. Communications were wiped out, and over four hundred industrial sites were turned to rubble. 853,000 citizens were unemployed, 850,000 technically unemployed, and 80,000 were directly affected by the raids. Estimates regarding the amount of damage varied. *The Economist* suggested that it amounted to U.S. $85 billion, while Yugoslav estimates placed the damage at $215 billion.

Though the intensity and duration of the raids were denounced throughout the international community, the western alliance persisted, and when a reporter challenged U.S. President Bill Clinton on the issue, he replied that the U.S. only goes to war when it plans to win.

The Council of the European Union then banned about three hundred Serbs from its territories, including the Miloševićs, their children, daughter-in-law, and Milošević's brother, Borislav, the ambassador to Russia. It was a clear signal that the EU would no longer tolerate the Milošević regime, and on 27 May 1999 the International War Crimes Tribunal in The Hague issued indictments against Milošević, Milutinović, the army chief of staff, Dragoljub Ojdanić, and Serbia's minister of police, Vlajko Stojiljković, for crimes against humanity and war crimes committed in Kosovo. Milutinović's indictment came as a surprise, since he had little or no authority. In the West he had been regarded at first as a potential ally who could undermine Milošević, but when it was time for him to act, he proved to be far too intimidated by Milošević.

Meanwhile not a single Albanian leader was indicted, nor any statesman or military commander under whose authority Serbia was being destroyed and its innocent civilians killed.

Živadin Jovanović, the minister of foreign affairs, informed Milošević of the indictments during an informal visit by Greece's former prime minister, Constantine Mitsotakis. Milošević reacted as though he wasn't worried, and said that he had been threatened with an indictment before the Dayton conference, but still made sure that western troops in Bosnia weren't attacked. "And now," he continued, "they'll need me to ensure the safety of their troops in Kosovo." However, subsequent events would prove that the indictment was in fact meaningful to him, and he soon told Russia's prime minister, Victor Chernomerdin, who acted as a conduit between Washington and Belgrade, that he was ready to negotiate.

On 2 June 1999 Chernomerdin and Finland's president, Martti Ahtisaari, landed in Surčin, at the only airport near Belgrade that hadn't been destroyed. U.S. Deputy Secretary of State Strobe Talbott didn't wish to meet with Milošević, nor did he need to, since Chernomerdin and Ahtisaari arrived in Belgrade with yet another ultimatum. Milošević greeted them in the White Palace. The indictments weren't mentioned, and Milošević was asked to surrender. Ahtisaari bluntly told him that unless he signed, the raids would continue and be followed by an invasion. "Sooner or later," he said, "you'll have to give in." Milošević then enquired whether the UN or NATO would control Kosovo. Ahtisaari replied that it would be the UN, upon which Milošević proposed to resume the meeting the following day, after Serbia's parliament had considered the matter.

Milošević was ready to sign, and since either Drašković or Šešelj's support was enough to provide him with a majority in parliament, he alone would determine the outcome. Chernomerdin and Ahtisaari accepted the delay, and Milošević met with his wife and other party leaders around midnight. It was a sombre occasion. Milošević acknowledged that there was no way out except to accept the ultimatum, and the following day parliament endorsed his position: 136 members voted to end the war, 74 Radical Party members opposed, and 3 members abstained.

After seventy days, on 9 June 1999 at 10:30 P.M., it was announced that the NATO raids were finally over. The last air-raid warning – and there had been 292 in Belgrade – sounded at 6:29 P.M. An RTB announcer stated that Milošević and Yugoslavia had won a "great victory." It was a huge relief, both for Milošević, who feared that the Americans would see their campaign through, and for the alliance, which had encountered increasing opposition to the raids. Strobe Talbott even acknowledged that managing tension stemming from the campaign's intensity, both within NATO and with the Russians, had become a problem, and that it would have been difficult to proceed had Milošević not surrendered when he did. Meanwhile Milošević urged the nation to enjoy the onset of peace, the Socialist Party announced that "the nation's freedom, dignity and honour" were preserved, Washington announced that the war had exemplified the "efficiency of combining diplomacy and force," and NATO's general secretary, Xavier Solana, said it was a "great day for the alliance, justice, and the people of Kosovo."

All Yugoslav regimes, beginning with the monarchy established in 1918, brought about the tragedy in Kosovo, which Milošević then precipitated. During the 1980s there had been talk of dividing the province, and in 1992 Dobrica Ćosić mentioned the idea to Cyrus Vance and David Owen, asking that it be included in their plan to end the war in Bosnia. Vance showed interest but felt that it was too early to act on the matter, and though Washington later presented the idea to Milošević, his popular support depended on Serbia's hegemony over Kosovo, and he refused to even consider the option.

Given a choice between accepting the West's humiliating terms, and bombardment, Milošević chose the latter, and was ultimately forced to accept terms that were more humiliating than those originally proposed. The West then established a military presence in Kosovo, and the Yugoslav Army and the Serbian police withdrew. Kosovo's borders with Albania and Macedonia were subsequently opened, and KLA troops, followed by tens of thousands of Albanians, entered the province.

Six hundred and ten years after the Serbs' defeat at Kosovo Polje, the province was lost, and *The Times* of London concluded that Kosovo had become a western colony. With the JNA and Serbian police no longer in the province, the KLA began to appropriate Serbian homes, land, hospitals, schools, and businesses and took over municipal administrations throughout the province.

Age-old hatreds culminated in murder, looting, extortion, and revenge. Within three months more than four hundred Serbs were killed, and the fate of approximately five hundred victims of abduction remains unknown. Fifty thousand Serbian homes were burned down, and sixty-two Orthodox churches were either destroyed or heavily damaged – including the Church of the Holy Virgin dating from 1315, which was turned to rubble. All Serbian books were burned, and the murders of sixty-five Albanians who had sided with Serbs were condoned by Hasim Taci. General Michael Jackson, the UN commander in Kosovo, noted that the Albanians were settling old scores with the Serbs, and American State Department spokesman Jamie Rubin remarked that no one had ever promised that Kosovo would turn into Switzerland overnight: this was, after all, the Balkans.

Over one million Albanian refugees returned from Albania and Macedonia, and approximately 200,000 Serb, Montenegrin, and Roma Kosovars were forced to abandon the province with whatever meagre possessions they could carry or fit into their vehicles. Except for a few rare exceptions, local members of the Serbian regime weren't among them, having had the means to purchase new lives for themselves before the Albanian onslaught. No more than 100,000 Serbs remained in Kosovo, a small minority that refused to abandon their homes, and risked humiliation, brutal oppression, and death. They might as well have been in a concentration camp.

The West's aggression was justified as a means of ending the Serbs' ethnic cleansing of Albanians but resulted in Albanians cleansing the province of Serbs. The Serbs were accused of genocide, but no other European nation in recent memory had endured a plight similar to theirs. And while their massive exodus was in progress, the U.S. Senate declared that Serbia was a terrorist state.

Meanwhile Mirjana Marković claimed that Yugoslavia's place among nations was more prestigious than ever. The regime announced reforms and reconstruction, and celebrated its victory. According to Milošević, the outcome was positive, and to further his point, he, who in ten years hadn't awarded a single honour to himself or anyone else, decorated more than five thousand soldiers and civilians and awarded honours to most institutions, including the entire state-run media.

The opposition came back to life. Though Drašković had supported the regime during the war, he now criticized it and adopted a more realistic, conciliatory stance towards the West, and was promptly ousted from the Yugoslav vice-presidency.

The Church called for Milošević to "resign in the interests of the nation and for his own salvation," so that "a new leadership, acceptable in Yugoslavia and abroad" could take over. The idea of doing this never even occurred to Milošević. He wasn't able to leave Yugoslavia, understandably wouldn't turn himself in to The Hague tribunal, and refused to submit to the will of those he considered his subjects. In his mind, he could only resist, and a huge wall was built around his residence.

Citizens were exhausted, depressed, and fed up. After years of being subjected to the regime's endless lies and manipulations, the tragedy in Kosovo, NATO raids, and poverty had ensured that nothing would appease their dissatisfaction with both the regime and the self-serving, ineffectual opposition. At first it seemed that the regime was about to collapse, but those expectations proved false, and though prayers were said to avoid violence, the opposition's efforts to incite the mob signalled that more bloodshed was inevitable.

According to the regime, Serbs were either patriots or traitors, the latter being anyone who sought change. Army reservists demonstrated in a number of cities to demand their pay, which amounted to a few dollars for each day they had fought in the war. These heroes, as the regime had called them, were now being deprived of their rights, and many were unemployed, unable to feed their families, and disillusioned. It was a shocking outcome, but may well have put an end to Kosovo's mythical value among Serbs.

21

"He Is Finished!"

The twelve years of Milošević's rule were years of wars, isolation, humiliation, and misery. At the end of the twentieth century citizens of Yugoslavia were forced to stand in long lines, waiting for milk, cooking oil, and medications. Even those who wanted to bury their dead had to wait seven days. Life became cheap, and being a bodyguard was a rewarding profession. The bottom had been reached, yet the sinking continued. The regime resembled an incurable convalescent who refused to die.

Serbia was plagued with a dual affliction: the regime's contemptible position was accompanied by that of an equally worthless opposition, a pawn in Milošević's hands. People grumbled, increased their dissatisfaction, and prayed to God for deliverance. The poet Dragica Janković stood in front of the parliament building holding a big placard on which she had written:

U ime srpsta, pravde i mira
Zbaci Boze s trona dva vampira.
[For Serbia, justice, and peace,
From two vampires, oh God, give us release.]

And the youth gathered in the Otpor movement called on the leader to do his last service to the nation and follow in the footsteps of his parents: "Slobodan, kill yourself and save Serbia!"

After the bombing of Serbia and the occupation of Kosovo, the regime regained its strength. The opposition parties were paralysed, the people fearful and helpless. At that time the young, rebellious members of the Otpor movement were the regime's main headache. Their symbol was a fist, their objectives the toppling of the regime and a change in the political system. The regime responded predictably with persecution and mass arrests of Otpor members. Though these courageous young people, mostly university students, spent a total of 42,000 hours in jail, nothing could stop or sway them. Their energy, enthusiasm, and boldness helped raise the fighting spirit of the nation and would eventually lead to a general uprising.

When faced with momentous obstacles Milošević usually withdrew. His policy was to make concessions to the opposition from time to time and to conduct international relations in such a way as to always leave the door open for further negotiations. But all of that changed with the occupation of Kosovo and The Hague indictment labelling him an alleged war criminal. This meant an end to flights to Geneva, vacationing in Greece, and endless mind games with U.S. representative Richard Holbrooke. Milošević now left his home only for visits to his offices in the Palace of the Federation and the White Palace, where he gave audience to his faithful lackeys, trusted generals, and insignificant foreign visitors. Even his visits to other parts of Serbia were few and far between.

He lived a secluded life, but from his seclusion he fought fiercely to hold on to power. For him and his cronies, power became a guarantee of personal freedom, even physical existence. Even if he were not delivered to the international tribunal in The Hague, he would be facing bitter opponents in his own country. Nenad Čanak, one of the opposition leaders, during a political rally pointed to a lamppost in downtown Belgrade proclaiming, "That one is reserved for hanging Slobodan Milošević!" Serbia's leader was thus faced with the following options: extradition to The Hague, the gallows, going into hiding, or fighting on to maintain power. He chose the last, determined to rule at all costs.

In clinging to power, Milošević relied on brute force but at the same time, quite inexplicably, he believed that he had wide support among the people. His closest associates fed him only the information and analysis they believed he wished to hear. The official media glorified him with such praise as "His heroism marks the end of the twentieth century"; " he symbolizes bravery, honesty, respect for principles, determination, and patriotism"; "he is the new David of the twentieth century, the best protector from the evil forces trying to destroy us!" The general staff of the Yugoslav Army formally nominated him for the highest decoration of National Hero. The chief of staff explained the nomination: "Milošević's statesmanship and wisdom are admired by the entire peace-loving world, seeing in him a commander-in-chief and statesman unparalleled in modern times."

Milošević was proclaimed the "first patriot of Yugoslavia," and his wife, Mirjana, was elevated to the status of a principal theoretician "of the world movement against imperialism." The adoration of the "First Couple" became pathetic and even sickening. But the principal victims of this propaganda were Slobodan and Mirjana. They believed that everything told them was actually the voice of the people.

In their brazenness and arrogance they did not recognize the existence of an opposition. "All we have is a bunch of scoundrels, thieves, and weaklings bribed by the West" was Milošević's assessment, expressed at the Socialist Party Congress held in January 2000. This statement was taken as a signal for a mud-slinging competition among Milošević's loyalists. Opponents of the regime were NATO mercenaries, fascists, traitors, bloody collaborators of the aggressor, filth, murderers, spies, and deserters. But that was not all. Opposition leaders were singled out for "special treatment" and declared neurotic hooligans, homosexuals, failed politicians, and drug addicts. Mirjana Marković liked to refer to them as "men and women with bizarre tendencies and hormonal afflictions."

In such a frenzied atmosphere Milošević made a fatal decision, one that was at the same time challenging, brazen, and risky. During the summer of 2000 he decided to change the constitution of Yugoslavia and have himself re-elected by popular vote, not by parliament as was previously the case. This decision was immediately followed by a call for early elections, almost ten months before his term was to expire. Milošević was certain of victory. He told the army chief of staff that he was sure of winning 70 per cent of the vote. So confident was he that he ordered the restoration of his former official residence, hit and partially destroyed by two missiles, convinced that he would again be the tenant. His wife oversaw every detail of the restoration, even choosing the colour of the curtains.

During the brief election campaign Milošević had nothing but disdain for the opposition. "We are facing a bunch of hares, rats, and hyenas set on making out of this proud nation a poodle, a toy for the foreign masters to play with when they are bored," he declaimed. To counter The Hague indictment, he organized a counter-trial in Belgrade. Forty-one leaders of NATO countries were tried in absentia for "war crimes against the civilian population." The courtroom-cum-legal-circus was freshly repainted and refitted for this extraordinary "trial," with the picture of Slobodan Milošević decorating the wall behind the judges.

The indictment was a hefty 192 pages long. The presiding judge explained the absence of the accused: "They have been duly called to stand trial, but they ignored this court or were, perhaps, afraid having to face their own conscience." After a trial of four days, all those accused – among them Bill Clinton, Madeleine Albright, Tony Blair, Jacques Chirac, Xavier Solana, and Wesley Clarke – were found guilty and sentenced to twenty years imprisonment. The regime loyalists who filled the courtroom gallery applauded the decision.

In the midst of the election campaign a man disappeared without trace, disturbing the public at large and showing yet again how cheap and unsafe life in Serbia was. He was no ordinary man. His name was Ivan Stambolić, the very person who lived to regret his former role as chief mentor and promoter of Milošević in his ascendancy to power. On the morning of 25 August Stambolić was out for his usual jog in a park close to his home. Then he vanished.

Why? Stambolić was in retirement, and although his critical views were made public from time to time, he was not a member of an opposition party, nor was he inclined to form a party of his own. The kidnapping took place during the heated campaign in which Milošević monitored the field of likely opponents. Stambolić's name was mentioned a few times, though not by Stambolić himself, nor did he give any indication that he would enter the race. But perhaps Milošević was fed the information that Stambolić was becoming "too active." As always, the words and actions of Mirjana Marković were an important signal of regime's plans. Just about the time of the kidnapping, she confided to a group of loyalists, "The opposition will not be a problem. We should be concerned about the ghost of the 8th Plenary Session [when Stambolić was ousted] affecting our own ranks."

The regime's media suggested that Stambolić was kidnapped by one or another of the Balkan mafias because of shady dealings he was involved with. The police washed their hands of any participation, and Milošević just kept silent about the whole affair. He gave no sign of being touched by the calamity that had befallen his former best friend. He didn't call Stambolić's wife to offer sympathy, though he knew her well, having spent many days and nights as a guest in their home. When Kiro Gligorov, until recently the president of Macedonia, called to ask about Stambolić's fate, Milošević opted for the mafia explanation. To this day the fate and whereabouts of Stambolić, or his remains, are unknown. Sadly, he was not there to celebrate the fall of a despised regime.

ELECTION DAY, 24 SEPTEMBER 2000

The only time that Milošević had won a clear majority was in the very first multi-party elections in 1990. He held on to power in subsequent elections either by stealing votes or splitting the opposition. But this time a miracle happened: eighteen parties of the opposition united into a common block. This surprised Milošević and delighted an electorate grown weary of bickering within the opposition. An atmosphere of "now or never" was created. Either the opposition stuck together and overthrew the regime, or Serbia was doomed to prolonged misery and international isolation.

In another precedent, the opposition parties were unanimous in choosing a candidate to run against Milošević. Vojislav Koštunica was the fortuitous choice, to the surprise of the regime and the public at large. Koštunica was the president of the Democratic Party of Serbia, a party that had never gained more than 6 per cent of the popular vote in previous elections. He appeared to be an unambitious, good-natured person, with mild manners. Private and fiercely protective of his personal life, he was a man who seemed better suited to academia than political battle. The word was that he communicated well in one-on-one situations or with a few people, but anything above that was "a crowd, which made him feel uncomfortable." In public polling before the forging of the coalition, only 4 per cent saw him as presidential material. At the same time, however, 60 per cent did not hold a negative attitude about the possibility of his becoming president. The West took note of him only when he became a presidential candidate.

Koštunica's nomination proved to be an excellent choice for the united opposition, and all that remained to be done was make the public aware of the man and his qualities. A serious, honest, principled politician, he was equally critical of Milošević and the West. This proved to be the winning combination, since the public at large was fed up with both Milošević and the western alliance involved in the senseless bombing of Serbia and the occupation of Kosovo. Koštunica was a convinced royalist and anti-communist, a believer and church-goer, a democrat and legalist, possessing a unique blend of nationalism and *real-politik*. He declared himself to be a "defensive nationalist." His lifestyle was modest: he lived in an apartment inherited from his parents and drove an older model of the national car, the Yugo. In stark contrast to many other politicians, he had no history of financial misdealings, no ghosts in his closets. His honesty was credible, and when he declared, "I give you my word that I will not change once I am in power," the people believed him.

The opposition parties did their very best to support Koštunica, but he himself exceeded all expectations during the campaign. Gone was the timid, shy, and reserved politician. He was everywhere, moving from town to town without bodyguards, mixing and mingling with the crowds, a reassuring smile on his face, his hand stretched out for a multitude of handshakes. At a rally in Kosovska Mitrovica, Milošević's cohorts threw eggs, apples, tomatoes, and even stones at him. Koštunica withstood all attacks with dignity and calm.

And then came victory. Koštunica was elected president of Yugoslavia in the first round. The opposition also won in almost all major cities and towns of Serbia. The coalition of the left, made up of Milošević's SPS and Marković's JUL, suffered a resounding defeat. But so did Šešelj's Radicals and Drašković's SRM, two parties that had traditionally wreaked havoc in the Serbian opposition. This time the electorate gave them the punishment they deserved – a welcome bonus to the sweet victory over Milošević.

But all was not over. In Serbia the casting of votes was less important than the counting of them. There Milošević was up to his old tricks – the stealing of votes. Inadequate control of voting in Kosovo by the opposition produced 5,500 votes for Milošević in Priština, a city with barely two hundred Serbs. In Glogovac, with no Serb residents, Milošević got 4,500 votes. In Serbica, where eighteen people cast their votes, Milošević got 1,093. And so on.

The opposition received another unexpected blow: the ruling party in Montenegro decided to boycott the elections. For a number of years Milo Djukanović, the president of Montenegro, had had the sympathy and wide-ranging support of the democratic opposition of Serbia because he stood up to Milošević's undemocratic regime. At the time he would say, "With a democratic Serbia – yes; under Milošević – never!" But eventually it became evident that this was just a good political ploy and that Djukanović was actually intimately committed to the course of independence for Montenegro. The champions of democracy in Montenegro suddenly became champions of opposing a common state with Serbia, irrespective of political changes that had occurred. What a metamorphosis! Three years before, Djukanović's party had supported the election of Milošević as president. Then Djukonović became a vocal critic of Milošević's regime. Ultimately he became a critic of a common state called Yugoslavia.

But in spite of stolen votes and Djukanović's boycott, the democratic opposition won a decisive victory. Koštunica won 54.66 per cent of the vote against Milošević's 35.01 per cent. The "Leader of All Serbs" was defeated even in Požarevac, his home town. Milošević was stunned. He couldn't believe or accept the possibility of defeat. If he hadn't known his associates so well, he might have thought they were joking. When he heard the news his first words reportedly were: "You idiots!" The idiots were the very same people who had lauded his idea of early elections, convincing him that victory was certain, defeat out of the question. One of the "idiots" had publicly proclaimed that Milošević would knock out Koštunica "100 per cent to zero."

Just as disbelieving of the election results was Milošević's wife. "It is not possible that this is a true expression of people's opinions," she cried. "This is a CIA conspiracy, aided by domestic traitors!"

But there was no time for mourning and licking of wounds. Something had to be done quickly to "set things right again." Milošević regained his composure and instructed his lackeys to "organize a recount of the vote," which would buy time and delay the handing over of power. Two options were considered. The first was to recount the votes in such a way as to reduce Koštunica's total below 50 per cent, which would then secure a second round between the two. The second option was to declare the elections void and call new ones later, at an unspecified date. In the event, the first option was chosen. The Milošević-controlled election commission announced the final tally: Koštunica, 48.96 per cent; Milošević, 38.62 per cent. Overnight Koštunica was robbed of hundreds of thousands of votes.

Milošević decided not to give over the reins of power, thus sinking hopes that the transition would be peaceful. The opposition had a big decision to make. Should it accept the leader's conditions, enter new negotiations, and admit its own weakness, or defend the election results and respond in kind – that is to say, with force of its own? It was not an easy choice. Accepting Milošević's game and compromising with him would disappoint and disillusion the voters. Not accepting his proposal for a second round could lead to a bloody confrontation, this time pitting Serbs against Serbs.

The opposition did not hesitate. Facing them was a despised regime, while backing them were the people, ready to defend their vote and the election results. For the people of Serbia the choice was not between the regime and the opposition but between the regime and life in dignity. If the outcome could not be secured legally, it would have to be secured through a mass uprising and civil disobedience. Practically overnight Serbs rose in great numbers, flawlessly guided by the opposition leaders. The fire of revolt was lit by the coal-miners of Kolubara who staged a walkout, and the flame soon spread throughout Serbia. Roads were blocked, schools and shops were closed, workers went on strike in 80 per cent of state-owned enterprises. Strike committees were formed even in the regime-controlled media. The unity of the people in revolt was incredible. When the police tried to take over the Kolubara mines from the 7,000 striking workers, in no time at all the miners were joined by about 30,000 citizens who made a threatening circle around the police, forcing them to back off.

Milošević was agitated but still did not comprehend the enormity of the revolt and the danger he was facing. He made a public appearance on 30 September at the promotion of the graduating class of the Military Academy. He was convinced that the army would stand by him, and the chosen venue for his speech was meant to be a clear threat to the mutinous people. In a surprising and unusual move, he decided to address the nation again the following day. He looked fatigued and spoke as if he were disappointed with his own people, led by the opposition into an abyss. "Citizens should know that by taking part in [this] subversive activity, the goal of which is foreign domination, they bear a historic responsibility for the subsequent loss of control over their own lives," he said. "My conscience would not be at peace if I were to withhold from my people what I thought of their fate, and if that fate were to be imposed by outsiders." He went on to warn the citizens that external and internal forces of darkness had joined hands against Serbs and Serbia, and only he could guarantee their freedom and independence: "It should be clear to everyone that they [the West] are not attacking Serbia because of Milošević, but Milošević because of Serbia."

THURSDAY, 5 OCTOBER 2000

Over the previous week or so, the countryside and smaller towns of Serbia had been taken over by the opposition. The final act was to unfold in Belgrade, the seat of Milošević's regime. The opposition called for a rally "of all Serbia" in the capital. But this time the objective was not only to meet in protest, wave flags and placards, make appropriate speeches, and blow whistles and horns. The goal was to topple Milošević's pyramid of power.

Everything was carefully planned. Up to 300,000 people were expected in Belgrade from other towns of Serbia. The roles were divided among various groups: demonstrators from Niš were to take over the parliament building; those from Čačak, the state television; from Novi Sad, the federal building; from Šabac, the airport; and from Pančevo, the headquarters of the Belgrade police. Spontaneous events did not allow for the exact execution of the plan, but all the objectives were met.

The opposition and the demonstrators were uncertain of the attitude of the police and the army and how they would respond. Would they allow themselves to be (ab)used? The leaders of the opposition had contacts with some high-level police officers who assured them that their units would not blindly follow the dictates of the regime and its head. Even the police were by now impressed with the widespread revolt, and many decided to play it safe and go with the flow. Some units refused to travel to Belgrade to act as a security buffer for the regime. The officers of the elite paratroop unit stationed in Niš made it known that they would not partake in any "dirty work" to defend the regime.

The opposition leaders finally decided nothing could be gained by words and talk and that the battle needed to be fought with other means, including the use of force. Special units were assembled of trained men armed with adequate gear for street-battle, ranging from small arms and bullet-proof vests to Molotov cocktails. Communication between these groups was maintained through twenty-five satellite phones. Every group was aware at all times of what the others were doing.

By 5:30 A.M. on the fateful day the twenty-kilometre-long column of vehicles coming from Čačak was approaching Belgrade. It was made up of buses, cars, trucks loaded with stones, and of earth-movers and other equipment needed to remove potential barricades. Sitting proudly on a flat-bed truck was a bulldozer that would later become a symbol of the resistance. At the head of the column was the fiery mayor of Čačak, surrounded by his strongmen: policemen who had switched sides, karate and judo combatants, veterans of campaigns in Kosovo and Bosnia. It will never be known how many carried arms, but they were determined to use them if the need arose. There would be no going back without victory.

Several police blockades were set up on instructions from Milošević's minister of police: "The demonstrators must be stopped at all cost from entering Belgrade. Throw hand grenades at the oncoming vehicles if you have to." But the police did nothing. They stood aside and watched in disbelief as the heavy earth-moving equipment broke through one barricade after another.

Chanting "Insurrection!" and "Rebellion!" they entered Belgrade and, using the main city arteries, reached the big plaza in front of the parliament building. That was the beginning of the end, the final forty-eight hours of Milošević's regime.

By 1:00 P.M. the streets and squares of central Belgrade were packed with people. Above them circled a lone helicopter, annoying and spooking the crowd, informing the army general staff about the size of the demonstrations. Anywhere between 700,000 and a million. Who could tell? Who could think of resisting such a force?

The first attempt to take over parliament was suppressed by police batons and tear gas. The police did not use firearms. One could almost feel that their resistance was feeble, that they were seeking understanding and sympathy from the crowd and were in no way ready to die for Milošević's regime. Milošević had counted on the police. His loyal minister of police, originating from the same town as Milošević, called up all available units. The biggest hopes were with the Red Berets, an elite corps of fifteen hundred legionnaires specially trained for street fighting. These were the men who were in the thick of fighting in Bosnia and Kosovo. Then there was the special anti-terrorist brigade as well as the paramilitary formations, veterans of many campaigns in previous wars. All in all, it was an army of about five thousand battle-hardened, ruthless men.

But Zoran Djindjić, the opposition campaign manager, was in contact with the Red Berets. He was given strong assurances that this highly professional unit would not intervene, provided that demonstrators did not fire first at the police and the army. Furthermore, he was assured that the Red Berets would protect the demonstrators if they came under fire from either police or army units. "They will then have to deal with us, not the students," were the reassuring words of the Red Berets' commander, whose final comment was, "Milošević is finished."

By 4:00 P.M., after about three hours of pushing and shoving, several thousand demonstrators broke through the cordon of five hundred police and entered the parliament building. Among those inside, elated with victory, were also some overcome by anger and fury. They ransacked parliament and set a fire that burned a small part of the historic building. As thick smoke gushed out a few windows, the demonstrators left the building with "souvenirs." A young man was seen carrying the president's chair on his back. Of a number of valuable paintings that hung on parliament's walls, none remained. They were written off as "the price of revolution."

At certain points in the city the police still tried to maintain a defensive perimeter, but their hearts weren't in it. More and more police joined the crowd, handing over their firearms. Others fled to save their skins. The demonstrators gained confidence and courage. They overtook one of the police stations in central Belgrade, taking away all 499 firearms they found in the armoury.

Milošević had placed great faith in his police, for ten years a main pillar of his power. But after the NATO aggression on Yugoslavia, the glory had gone to the army. He felt sure the army would stand by him, come hell or high water – at least that was what he was told by the generals who sought his favour and endorsement. In return they were rewarded with promotions, decorations, and villas in the exclusive Dedinje suburb of Belgrade.

Milošević's favourite among the generals was Nebojša Pavković, a capable troop commander, intelligent, crafty, and endlessly ambitious. He was promoted to army chief of staff after the Kosovo campaign. Pavković was often together with his commander-in-chief and was favoured as well by Mirjana. Pavković made a promise that he would prevent civil war, and the leader and his wife thought that he meant that he would defend the regime from insurrection. A few days before the elections Pavković announced that 24 September would be "D-Day ... the army will prevent the takeover of power in the streets." After such a statement many in the opposition also felt that Pavković would use the army to stop the political demonstrations.

During the morning of 5 October, Milošević called Pavković several times, urging him to deploy the army because "the police are unable to resist the violence on their own." The general's response was encouraging. He promised that a "tank unit would be activated immediately." Yet time went by and no tanks or other army units appeared. Pavković was informed that the police had all but collapsed. He was monitoring the situation very carefully and must have been fully aware that the disposition in the army rank and file was similar to that of the police. By ordering an attack he would risk mutiny within his own ranks. Thus he did nothing. He testified later in an interview that the idea of using the army "never crossed his mind." It later leaked out that the day before the demonstrators gathered in Belgrade, a group of generals held a meeting in secret and decided to defy any order to use troops against the people. One of the generals summed up the decision: "Milošević lost the elections. Let him find his own way out and leave us out of it." This decision of influential generals must have reached the opposition leaders as well. During the whole day no one saw or heard from the minister of defence, General Ojdanić. He wasn't in his office nor was he at home. The military police found him in a pub later in the evening when it was all over.

Around 4:30 P.M., after having successfully stormed parliament, the mass of demonstrators moved towards the state television, a hated and despised symbol of the regime. Security forces around the building, still with a spark in them, tried to fend off the demonstrators with tear gas, batons, and rubber bullets. A young demonstrator threw a flaming cardboard box through a window, setting off a fire that would engulf half the building. The bulldozer mentioned earlier finished the job by breaking through the main entrance. An hour before, the panicked director had called Milošević asking for help. "Hold on," Milošević replied. "Pavković is sending the army."

Soon after, all major state institutions were taken over by the protesters. The worst fate befell the directors of various state media institutions. The state television director was beaten up on the sidewalk, the director of an evening newspaper was grabbed by the workers and was about to be dumped like a sack of potatoes into a vat of paint. Fortunately he fainted, and that saved him. The director of *Politika*, the oldest newspaper in the Balkans, fled his office via the fire escape.

The burned-out state television building and the partially demolished parliament are the sad part of this story. There were also three casualties, none from police force. A young woman's fall from a truck proved fatal, an elderly man died of heart failure, and a third succumbed to a stroke. It was probably the most peaceful and orderly people's uprising in modern history. Yet the consequences are and will continue to be far-reaching.

Church bells tolled the victory, and the streets were full of joyous people hugging and kissing and wishing each other "a happy freedom!" At 9:10 P.M. after several hours of silence, TV Belgrade came back to life with a new face and an announcement: "This is the program of the new Radio-Television of free Serbia." If Milošević was watching, he must have realized that his rule was now in great danger. But he wasn't quite ready to give up. During the night he gave an order for a showdown with the leaders of the opposition. Mirjana Marković's chief of security took a letter to General Pavković containing names of the opposition leaders who were to be liquidated. According to Parković he replied that he was unable to carry out that specific order. Milošević's angry reply was, "In that case I will send the secret state security units and the Red Berets to finish the job." Clearly he was unaware that the Red Berets had switched sides.

In the small hours of the night, President-Elect Koštunica went to bed for a few hours of sleep. In an interview a week later he said he did so with a feeling that his sleep would be interrupted by the police coming to arrest him.

FRIDAY, 6 OCTOBER 2000

I too went to bed very late. By 5:00 A.M. I was already up again, roaming the streets of Belgrade. They resembled the aftermath on a battlefield or perhaps more appropriately, the scene after an uproarious carnival. Tonnes of paper littered the ground, along with bottles and other trash, iron rods, sticks, stones, other discarded "weapons," and a few burned-out automobiles. The police were nowhere to be seen.

In front of the parliament building hundreds of protestors from Čačak were celebrating victory with a band of musicians. The park across from the parliament looked like a refugee camp. People from the interior without relatives in Belgrade were enjoying a well-deserved rest. They had no intention of going back home before Milošević publicly conceded defeat. Many shop windows displayed a simple message: "He is finished!" In the centre of

Belgrade a perfume shop owned by Milošević's son, Marko, appropriately called Scandal, was totally demolished. All that was left was the lingering scent of perfume and the graffiti, "Go and complain to your daddy."

The day of joy passed while the opposition attempted to consolidate and legalize its rule. "Crisis teams" took over several institutions, while those loyal to the regime watched in fear, unsure of what to expect. General Pavković met with President-Elect Koštunica late in the afternoon and congratulated him on his election victory. The general then practically forced Milošević to meet with Koštunica. Koštunica suggested the federation building, the official seat of government. Milošević, concerned about his safety, instead insisted they meet in his residence. Koštunica yielded.

During the many years of his rule Milošević had met with all the leaders of the opposition except Koštunica. He had never showed anything but disdain for Koštunica's party. During this, the first encounter between the two, both men were tense and reserved with only a cordial "good evening," while Milošević expressed regret at not having had a chance to meet Koštunica before. The general left the house, allowing the former and the new president time alone for an hour. Milošević admitted defeat and expressed concern for the safety of his family and close collaborators. He seemed dejected and unfocused. At one moment, as if totally forgetting his predicament, he started talking of his son's childhood.

Finally at 10:40 P.M. Milošević addressed the nation to say that he had "just received the official election results and the information that Vojislav Koštunica had won the presidential election." He congratulated the victor and wished the people of Yugoslavia success in the forthcoming period. Though visibly depressed, he did not have the courage to open his heart. He acted and spoke as if this were just a normal, routine change of power. He even thanked those who voted against him because, as he said, they relieved him of a weight that he "had carried for ten years." He went on to add that it was good for his party to take a break from responsibilities: "I always said a party cannot show its full strength and all its qualities if it is not in opposition for a while."

He concluded, "Personally, because of the heavy burden of responsibility that I bore for ten years, I intend to rest a while, to spend more time with my family, above all with my grandson. Then I will continue strengthening my party."

At the same time Mirjana's faithfuls informed the public that her party was "strong and energized and will be ready and at the starter's block in the next elections."

SATURDAY, 7 OCTOBER 2000

This was the day when Milošević's rule officially came to an end. The first meeting of the new federal Parliament took place in a congress centre because of the damage done to the parliament building. The inauguration of the new president, Vojislav Koštunica, was marked with a modest celebration to which all Socialist deputies came in buses. Milošević was not there. He and his wife probably watched the live coverage of the swearing-in ceremony, finally realizing that they had lost. Not only did they lose power but they lost peace and quiet in the family. Suffering a nervous breakdown, their daughter, Marija, shot and killed a dog belonging to her neighbour and old friend. Their son, Marko, took flight under an assumed name to Bejing via Moscow. Marko was hated so much in Požarevac where he had lived and terrorized the community that he could not return there. His security until he boarded his plane was provided by no less an authority than the chief of the Serbian secret police.

A tragic chapter in the history of Serbia came to an end. Its chief protagonist, Slobodan Milošević, never received its highest official honour – the Order of the National Hero, weighing over 600 grams, made of gold and studded with five diamonds on the tips of a star, was to be officially presented to him after the elections as a crowning moment for all his victories. It remained in the vaults of the National Bank.

And while Serbia celebrated victory, exclaiming with joy, "It's over, it's over," and "He is finished, he is finished," Slobodan Milošević and Mirjana Marković remained in their hideout, the official residence of the president. The new leadership agreed to offer Milošević army protection over and above his personal bodyguards. Television and telephone were the couple's only contacts with the outside world. But though Milošević was down, he was not out. He encouraged his followers and loyalists, cheering them on and boosting their morale, assuring them that all was not lost.

22

Slobodan and Mirjana: A Retrospective Portrait

Devoted as Slobodan Milošević and Mirjana Marković have always been to each other, their personalities, characters, and politics are dramatically different. According to her, he has never been as committed to an ideology as she is, and "would never say something like 'I am ready to die for socialism ... or internationalism.'"

Despite his communist background, Milošević's one true allegiance has been to power. Having become a member of former Yugoslavia's Communist Party on 15 January 1959, he was a "good communist," and his peers in the Belgrade leadership even called him "Little Lenin." He also became a nationalist, and incited war but then struggled for peace. There are simply no ideals to which he is committed. Though he embraced the Serbian cause, his nationalism was never extreme and vicious. None of his speeches or comments betrayed even the slightest hint of xenophobia. While Tudjman, whose grandchildren are half Serbian, thanked God that his mother hadn't been Jewish or Serbian, Milošević's sole motivation in inciting nationalism was to strengthen his hold on power. His family hails from Montenegro, but he never mentioned his Montenegrin roots, and called himself a Serb. Beyond that he gave no indication that he felt either Serb or Montenegrin. Also, he was more nostalgic for former Yugoslavia than were the other national leaders and held on to its insignia, anthem, and holidays. While Tudjman and Izetbegović became captives of their nationalism, Milošević remained a staunch Yugoslav and fondly recalled the Tito era as the best years of his life.

One could say he had friends, but they were only to be found among his political allies. He was truly close and loyal to no one but his family. Anyone else was either for him or against him, with no middle ground. He exploited both communists and anti-communists, nationalists and Yugoslavs, patriots, chetniks, intellectuals, the church, and Bosnian Serbs, and repudiated all of them once they were no longer of use.

Writers, academicians, and scholars helped him to secure the leadership during the national awakening, believing that he would be their instrument, but he turned his back on them as soon as they became a liability. To his mind intellectuals were self-aggrandizing fools. For example, while he was still president of the Belgrade Party, he once asked what "two or three hundred writers" could possibly represent as compared to "twenty thousand workers," and when two highly respected academicians visited him to complain of a "dramatic" situation in which the Serbian Academy was unable to agree on a new president, he dismissively asked whether they truly believed that their choice mattered.

His dealings with the church were similar. Though his father was a theologian, he has never been religious and has shown no desire to turn to religion; yet he has approached the church whenever it could be of use. In wake of the 1991 demonstrations, he visited Hilandar and later deceitfully obtained Patriarch Pavle's approval to represent the Bosnian Serbs at the Dayton Conference. "So help me God, Your Holiness, I am speaking to you in all honesty, as a son to his parent," he declared. But when the church began to question his policies, he bluntly ignored the patriarch's requests for a meeting.

Milošević couldn't stand the Bosnian Serbs and incited their uprising only in an attempt to broaden his leadership. He humiliated their leaders, calling them "the Bosnian dolts," and once told Karadžić: "I'll give you a salt block, and then you go lick it." His reactions were just as vulgar when Bosnian Serbs were simply mentioned. Richard Holbrooke once referred to them as "your friends," to which Milošević replied, "They aren't my friends, they're shit." And meeting with Holbrooke while the Bosnians were being bombarded, he never once mentioned their plight, a lack of empathy that Holbrooke found appalling.

If politicians are to be judged by their ability to remain in power no matter how disastrous their policies, Milošević is a master. He cemented his hold on the leadership by inciting war, and then, having been forced to surrender, turned his failure into a political philosophy that further glorified his leadership. Once he even told a reporter from the *Washington Post* that he was proud of the role he had played in defending Serbia's interests. "My conscience is clear," he said, "and there is nothing I specifically regret."

He has never tolerated competition, and was particularly irked if anyone but his wife was spoken of as his successor. The only time he allowed anyone to run against him in elections for the Socialist Party leadership was in 1990, when Radmila Andjelković, who was later richly rewarded, obediently agreed to be the losing candidate.

He has always taken great pride in his leadership and was extremely offended whenever it was called into question, no matter how innocently. For instance, after once being reminded that his presidential term was nearing an end, he angrily suggested that he would remain in power for as long as he wished. His sense of entitlement surpassed all bounds, and he never considered the possibility of being mistaken, let alone guilty. Yet beneath a facade of superiority and control, he has shown himself to be a typically insecure depressive, a man whose greatest fear is to lose what he has accomplished.

Contrary to all other twentieth-century Serbian leaders, who, in the words of Professor Milovan Milanović, made efforts to "tie the Serbian dinghy to the European steamer," Milošević has confronted the powerful in an inevitable slide towards disaster. Extremely impulsive, he has never made any effort to strike a balance between what he wants and what can actually be accomplished. Many of his decisions have been poorly considered, either premature or devastatingly belated, and lacking in foresight. He has never seriously applied himself to government; he is unpredictable and lacks vision because he doesn't subscribe to any ideals. But having drawn worldwide attention to himself, he has concluded that he is surely a great man.

Though he often failed to grasp obvious trends, such as the global shift away from communism, he always somehow managed to emerge unscathed or even strengthened from the worst of predicaments. He was a master of political intrigue and deceit, "a genius of petty manoeuvring," according to Bosnian historian Mehmet Ekmedžić. And western leaders, who wrote him off but then realized that he was irreplaceable, could only agree.

Half measures were alien to Milošević; he was either unyielding or resigned, and the only way to influence him was to threaten force, which he respected and feared. Encouraged by his support among Serbs, he kept waging battles and collecting enemies in an effort to achieve greater influence. But eventually, facing defeat and fearing its consequences, he yielded more than was necessary. Yet he never fully surrendered, and his concessions only lasted while he recovered from his losses. He held on to the leadership through electoral fraud, systematic deceit, corruption, brutality, and an inferior opposition, but he ultimately survived in power because toppling his regime wasn't one of the international community's primary objectives.

Though he feared the Americans, he thought at first he could stand up to them. But he liked the Russians, even though he was hypocritical towards them. For instance, he sought Yeltsin's assistance, but supported his communist opposition. And though he didn't trust Yeltsin and failed to inform Yevgeni Primakov of his decision to schedule a referendum regarding foreign intervention in Kosovo on the eve of NATO's attack, he was frequently dismayed that despite the Russians' tremendous power, they submitted to the Americans. One can only imagine to what use he himself might have put such power.

There have been few situations Milošević wasn't capable of withstanding, however difficult, but his willingness to endure often made matters worse. Though his arrogance and extreme self-confidence frequently led to mistakes, his lust for power has been by far the greatest source of our misery.

Milošević thrived on chaos, which he created in order to demonstrate that he alone could restore order; however, the order he established was neither just nor legal. He never accounted for his actions and tolerated a bare minimum of democratic discourse. He drew all power to himself, was preoccupied with each and every detail of government, and remained aloof from ordinary

Serbs, the opposition, and even his own party, which he undermined in order to accommodate YUL.

Having acquired more power than any Serbian king ever had, he felt there was no need to pretend that the nation's institutions were in control of the country, and government officials both accepted and paid ridiculous homage to his autocratic nature. For instance, when Yugoslav Prime Minister Radoje Kontić was asked by reporters whether negotiations with the international community were being conducted by Milošević or by the minister of foreign affairs, Kontić replied, "The most intelligent individual is negotiating: Slobodan Milošević."

Milošević's most striking characteristic has always been his complete lack of trust. He keeps everything to himself, and quoting an American general, once said that if his hair knew what his intentions were, he'd have to shave it off. He rarely commits anything to writing, and people who take notes annoy him. Verbal agreements, with no witnesses, are more to his liking. During a meeting with U.S. President Clinton's advisor Robert Frasure, Milošević was alone, and when an agreement they had reached needed to be written up, it soon became apparent that no typists were on duty.

When he is under pressure, Milošević feels a need to fortify himself with alcohol. The American press reported that while he was negotiating for Bosnian territory in Dayton, he asked to be brought some whisky, and the territory in question, the Goradže corridor, thus became known as the "whisky corridor." Dobrica Ćosić recalls a similar experience: during the Vance-Owen phase of the peace process, Milošević asked for a drink and swallowed it in one gulp. Alcohol relaxes him and makes it easier for him to make decisions. He has a passion for firearms, even though he has never found himself in a situation where he had to use one. He carried one before it became the norm for Serbian officials, back when he was president of the Belgrade Party, and both of his children share his passion.

Reading bores him, and the only sources he trusts are his wife and the police. But he is highly interested in the occupations of his associates and opposition, and through surveillance has ensured that he knows more about them than they know themselves. One

of his great pleasures is to catch them lying. Although his informants had told him the exact amount of a mortgage one of Karić's
companies had extended to Drašković on his apartment, Milošević
mercilessly probed Karić for the same information. "More, Bogoljub, more," he kept repeating, until Karić told him the truth.

Milošević always insisted that his party associates address him
as "Comrade." "I'm not Mister," he said, "but Comrade!" He
even addressed the prior at Hilandar as "Comrade," but also liked
his people to call him "Chief." "President" is only a temporary
title, while "Chief" is permanent, even hereditary.

He can be both taciturn and extremely talkative. During the
war, splayed out on a sofa, he held forth for hours, but he has
always been able to avoid saying too much, never making statements that commit him to more than he is prepared to give, and
he remains silent when silence serves him best. For instance,
during the two-day session of the Serbian Party leadership in 1986
when his nomination to the presidency was at stake, he barely
spoke a word. A clear indication that he is under pressure is when
he evasively digresses or speaks in incomplete sentences. In any
case, both he and the other leaders of former Yugoslav republics
were only honest when it was convenient. "They look straight at
you and lie," Lord Owen once noted.

But in contrast to Franjo Tudjman, with whom UN secretary
general for the Balkans Karl Bildt once said he wouldn't care to
socialize, Milošević is capable of endearing himself to others, and
diplomats have often noted that he is courteous, patient, and
attentive. He insists on sharing meals with his visitors and takes a
personal interest in them. And though he is an obstinate, difficult
man to negotiate with, he keeps his word.

He fears illness but has trouble keeping to a healthy diet.
Throughout their regime, he and Marković trusted only the physicians at Belgrade's military hospital, who once diagnosed him
with a condition that required him to bring his own meals to functions not held in his home or office. His diagnoses and general
state of health, as well as Marković's, were closely guarded state
secrets. Milošević also has never shown any interest in sports,
even as a spectator – he himself acknowledges that his only sports
involvement is his fondness for sportswear. His favourite attire
when he's not in his office are training suits and flip-flops.

In the right mood, he often sings from a wide repertoire of songs he knows by heart and is blessed with a good voice. He has delighted Russian delegations with passionate renditions of their songs and was reported to have been found leaning against a piano during the Dayton conference, crooning away. Contrary to what people in the West may think, the Butcher of the Balkans has a lyrical soul.

He never discusses important issues in public, and his rare speeches have been concise, taut, and peppered with easy-to-remember slogans and rhetorical phrases such as "no reasonable person can deny," "it needn't be repeated," and "beyond any doubt." But though he is in many ways a populist and behaves confidently in public, he is actually uncomfortable in a crowd and only appeared before one when it was necessary, usually during elections. Unlike his wife, who enjoys publicity, he avoided the press, especially photographers. He didn't hold press conferences, nor did he address the nation in moments of crisis, when many Serbs expected him to. Any statements he felt needed to be made were given to a few hand-picked reporters from *Politika* or RTB, usually after an important meeting, and represented his final word on the matter. And when he said that something had been emphasized during a meeting, he was always referring to his own position. His statements were often incomplete and deceitful; he alone provided information on his activities, and he alone was their judge and commentator.

No one recalls him either mingling spontaneously with citizens or displaying solidarity with victims of the war or any other disaster. However many coffins and wounded returned from Bosnia, he never once visited a hospital or a home or otherwise showed concern. When Serb refugees were fleeing the Croatian Army, he remained silent, and when he was told that one of his associates was having a hard time dealing with the death of his son, he replied, "I can't stand tears. I respect people who bury their fathers and go right back to work."

For many years Milošević gave the impression that he attached very little importance to symbols of power and honours, of which he only accepted two, both while former Yugoslavia was still intact. And though he frequently received tokens of appreciation, souvenirs, and honorary citizenships, he felt no need to reciprocate. This not only didn't bother most Serbs but strengthened his aura of charismatic leadership. That all changed after he was indicted by The Hague tribunal, when his leadership, freedom, and even his life began to hang by a thread. From that point he began to crave recognition and revelled in the flattery of his followers, who began to refer to him as the "leader of the free world." However, this development only occurred in a later phase of his career when he began his desperate struggle to remain in power.

Although Mirjana Marković has always been more open than her husband and constantly in the public eye, she is also more difficult to comprehend. Exceedingly ambitious, she presents herself as a fragile, shy, guileless intellectual who longs for a world in which malice and sorrow have no place. "I am a universalist. I like everyone," she once said.

She became a member of the Communist Party when she was sixteen, and despite its collapse, remains passionately devoted to its ideals. "The left is older than politics and political parties, older than the sciences," she has said, adding that "leftists are first and foremost good people, humble and courageous," certainly not "cowards." The fact that Serbia has become Europe's last communist bastion is more her doing than Milošević's.

Marković went along with the renaming of the Communist Party but didn't renounce its ideology: "What's important to me is that such a society remain within the realm of possibility. The name is secondary." Her mission was to liberate Europe through Marxism, and she initially took advantage of the widespread criticism she encountered as a platform upon which to build her own political career.

Easily upset, she loses control whenever her beliefs are called into question and never fails to denounce anti-communists. When Bogoljub Karić advised her to abandon communism, she accused him of being callous and ran out of the room in tears. And during a visit to Bucharest she asked Rumanian academicians why Adam Puslojić, an "anti-communist," was a member of their academy.

She constantly attempted to persuade the public that her "intellectual, professional, and moral" commitment to the liberation of oppressed peoples was part of her genetic makeup. In one article she commiserated with poor students who weren't able to go to "proms in Belgrade's luxurious Hyatt wearing gowns by famous Rome or Paris designers." But nothing, she consoled them, "is more beautiful than a dress sewn by one's own mother, and nothing more romantic than an evening spent under a starlit May sky, sitting in a park, by the river, wearing any old shoes, white espadrilles on bare feet, and the colourful kind of dress in which one sits on outdoor steps." Yet her own life and that of her entourage was quite different. Marković's Serbia was a place where the rich got richer and the poor could only hope for better times. Virtually none of her followers was poor, and most belonged to the nation's political and financial elite. Questioned about the wealth of her party's members, she replied that they weren't capitalists to begin with but when the nation "embraced capitalism," they were able to "fend for themselves."

Her compassion generaly ended wherever reality intruded. She isolated herself from the plight of ordinary Serbs, fell silent whenever they were hit by disaster, and never engaged her party's substantial wealth in an effort to provide relief, all of which contributed to her lack of appeal. Orthodox communists saw her as a hypocrite, anti-communists despised her, and almost everyone felt she was a spoiled, out-of-control shrew.

Given her commitment to communism, Marković was especially fond of former Yugoslavia, the Soviet Union, and China. As Yugoslavia was disintegrating, she remained convinced that Croats, Slovenes, Macedonians, Serbs, and Muslims were all members of a "future Yugoslav nation" and refused to abandon the idea, even when those groups themselves clearly indicated that it was repulsive. She adored the Soviets, believing that civilization was forever in their debt, and praised all aspects of their country – including their winter, an "ethnic phenomenon that has given that great nation strength throughout its history ... And when that strength awakens, it will change the world."

Marković often denounced nationalism, and though she supported the movement that brought her husband to power, she rejected claims that he himself was a nationalist and once told David Owen, whom Milošević had failed to convince otherwise, that he was not a nationalist because she wouldn't have married him if he were. In any case her support of the movement ceased when the Bosnian Serbs, whom she despised, became a liability. She spoke of them xenophobically, as though they were aggressive immigrants.

Though she has few female friends and considers herself an atypical woman, Marković feels that her gender is generally oppressed. She kept her maiden name, which she says is as much a part of her identity as her citizenship and birth date, and sees no reason to renounce it because she married. Milošević, whom she rarely refers to as "my husband," supports her, and once said that he himself would never have married a woman who would have changed her name. Furthermore, Marković insists on being addressed as "Comrade," and believes that a "woman who wishes to be a lady will never be human."

She also believes it is her mission to enlighten, educate, and moralize, and unlike Milošević, who only cares for power, she has an insatiable craving for recognition. She has been hailed as an academician, university professor, party leader, literata, scholar, and thinker. The state-run media, particularly *Politika*, presented her as a superhuman intellectual, claiming that her scholarly and literary achievements were incomparable. She was the "media's crown jewel ... one of the most significant and interesting figures among a global scholarly elite"; and her books clearly demonstrated that she was "profoundly committed to a better future for the people." Large sums were wasted to establish her political and scholarly eminence. Donors and agents were recruited and a fortune was spent to publish many translations of her books. Though there was no market for these translations, they were all acclaimed as best-sellers. Covered in praise and protected by her husband's authority and love, she herself began to believe that she was an extraordinary figure. Asked to explain the popularity of her books, she replied that she was one of few Serbian intellectuals who had attempted to explain Serbia, and that she also wrote beautifully. Her confidence grew in accordance with the praise she encountered. At one point her primary goal was to establish an anti-American alliance between Russia, China, Belorus, India, and Yugoslavia, and she asked "oppressed and injured" peoples throughout the global community to "resist neo-colonialism and strive toward internationalist ideals."

Marković could be as loving as she was spiteful, and was equally intense in either mode. She patiently nurtured her friendships, and tolerated more independence of thought in her friends than in Milošević. She invariably spoke of family and allies as honest, unselfish, wise, and beautiful individuals, and lavished rewards on them – particularly on her children, guaranteeing their comfortable lifestyles. On the other hand, she dismissed her detractors, who included the opposition, the independent press, and especially lapsed allies, as "envious and inferior philistines," "semi-literate commentators who can't even resist the temptation to pilfer toilet paper from hotel rooms," "alcoholics whose two-bit rags are financed by a foundation that specializes in meddling in the affairs of others" and "unstable, cowardly little troublemakers." Dismayed that the opposition's leaders weren't considered traitors, she wrote: "If worldwide standards and laws were applied, they would either be imprisoned within a week or, at best, would try to flee the country by night, like unmasked spies." Furthermore, she regarded them as freaks of nature. One of them she described as a "werewolf. He has horribly large and pointed teeth, can't fully close his mouth, and his eyes are so wicked he gives children nightmares."

Obsessed with bodily hygiene, to which she accorded political, ethical, and aesthetic significance, Marković viewed clean people as necessarily good, honest, and attractive and belonging to her party. Conversely members of the opposition were "frustrated men who never learned to bathe properly," and whose "cities are filthy remnants of their lootings." And as for their wives, Marković invariably claimed they suffered from "hormonal imbalances."

Extremely moody, her reactions were often unpredictable and aggressive, as is typical of individuals who cannot or will not control their anger. A former friend remarked that while it was possible to have a pleasant conversation with her, he always felt uncomfortable in her presence. Once when he offended her, she froze into a stare and ignored his attempts to resume their conversation. "I understood then that it was best for me to leave," he said, realizing that their friendship was over.

Marković breaks easily into tears. She shed tears of joy upon meeting her ideological soul-mates in China and tears of frustration whenever her ideals were challenged. According to her biographer, Ljiljana Djurović, she becomes particularly upset whenever Milošević forgets himself and interrupts her while she is combing her hair in front of a mirror, a "sacred ritual" during which she "stares into the abyss of her own existence." Not surprisingly, Milošević's interruptions have prompted her to question whether he still loves her.

Though she is extremely energetic and endlessly devoted to her ideals, she often seems troubled. Short in stature and overweight, she dresses conservatively, usually in black, as do many people who wish to be taken seriously. She covers her forehead with her hair, and in 1996 underwent some difficult cosmetic surgery. She often consults physicians about her psychological problems, their diagnoses shrouded in the utmost secrecy.

She never attends church and claims she is an atheist. Nevertheless, she is superstitious – she doesn't wear yellow barrettes in her hair because her daughter once failed a geography exam while wearing one. She wears a moonstone ring "because the moon is a planet that offers protection." She frequently consults astrologers, an interest now shared by her family, including her husband, and maintains she often says "with a little sorrow and some irony, that the stars are able to accomplish what governments cannot." But ultimately she approaches astrology as a parlour game in which she can tell her friends what she thinks of them.

Regardless of her communist atheism, she began to observe her maternal grandparents' Slava, the celebration of the feast of their patron saint, during the mid-1990s. And when Alexei II, the Russian Orthodox patriarch, presented her with a gilded icon representing St Nicholas, she prominently displayed it in her study, alongside her portraits of Tito and Lenin.

Throughout the time of their ascendancy, the Miloševićs' private life was fairly monotonous. They rarely went out, and fraternized only with their allies. They claim to be most at ease alone together, holding hands and striving to prolong the romance of their younger days – he her "perfect man," she his "perfect woman." She loves him because he loves her, and "suffers less" when she is with him. She encourages, reprimands, and completes him, and he returns her affection. He is extremely attentive and tender with her and selflessly yields to her frequently ill-advised demands. Though they both are middle aged, when among friends he never hesitates to acknowledge that he depends on her love. He says he has never cheated on her and was once outraged when a secretary made a sexual overture to him.

The Miloševićs clearly adore their children, but they have not been particularly involved parents, and to the outrage of ordinary citizens, allowed them to take advantage of their privileged estate. Marija and Marko both hated school. Marija started out in an academically oriented high school, attended technical and commercial ones, and eventually graduated from a school that prepared students for careers in the tourist industry. As far as her parents were concerned, she only needed to graduate. She then married a diplomat thirteen years her senior. The marriage quickly failed, and Marija announced that it had been "boring to be a diplomat's wife." She had discovered that she was most at ease among her bodyguards and preferred guns to jewellery. She felt that to "hold a baby in one hand and a gun in the other" would have been "too complicated."

Eventually Marija went into business, where there was money to be made. Thanks to her mother and Bogoljub Karić, she became the managing partner of Košava Radio and Television, named by her mother after a south-easterly wind that buffets the Serbian plains. According to Marković, the name was a "psychological metaphor." Marija's involvement in Košava wasn't as lucrative as her brother's ventures, but both of their careers marked a trend in which the children of Serbia's official elites exploited their connections and became wealthy.

Marko Milošević craved independence but has also taken full advantage of his situation to acquire an extravagant lifestyle. He likes nothing better than to flash a wad of bills in a bar, surrounded by bodyguards and women. He loves cars and firearms and is so entirely fascinated by martial prowess that he once accompanied a Serbian delegation to Israel as a bodyguard. Ill at ease in Belgrade, he often went to Greece and built a luxurious home in Požarevac with his "own money." People acquainted with the Serbian elites claim he is one of the wealthiest individuals in Serbia. He made no attempt to deny this and once showed his father a briefcase full of deutschmarks, to prove that he wasn't a nobody. Milošević was concerned but didn't make an issue of it, and frequently boasted to friends of Marko's success.

Both of the Miloševićs' children were staunch defenders of communism. Marko flew communist flags in front of his Požare-vac discothèque, and Marija walked out of the Belgrade premiere of Emir Kusturica's *Underground* because of its "anti-communist content." Once while her mother was describing the Soviet Union's collapse, she broke into tears, lamenting, "All that's left is China."

Both Marko and Marija were affected by others' intolerance of their parents' regime, which they invariably dismissed as envious, inferior, or malicious. Eventually they felt surrounded by enemies – especially Marko, whose reactions became increasingly violent. In autumn 1997 his bodyguards stood by as he brandished a semi-automatic and made patrons of a café bury their heads between their knees and remain still while he stuffed a young man who had apparently sneered at him into a closet, making him "count slowly to one hundred." As it turned out, his victim was not sneering at all, but had been disfigured in an automobile accident.

After numerous similar incidents the Democratic Party ad-dressed an open letter to Milošević asking him to restrain his son and to cease placing his children above the law. The Draškovićs published an article in which they condemned Milošević's chil-dren and wife, and Milošević decided that he would no longer even have coffee with Drašković. But Marković took the high road, implying that she and her children were too sophisticated to be understood by ordinary Serbs.

It was Marković who instilled in her children an hysterical combativeness. When a reporter portrayed Marko as an arrogant show-off who took advantage of his father's situation, he retali-ated in a style his mother was sure to have approved of, if indeed she didn't compose his reply herself: "With or without my father, I am still young, capable, intelligent, and handsome," he an-nounced. He then labelled his detractor as one of the "spies, traitors, hirelings, and other rodents society has rejected" and con-cluded that as a "young intellectual" there was no need for him to respond to the "political and moral dregs" of Serbian society.

Although the Miloševićs denounced crime, their entourage was full of shady characters and parasites. Members of the leadership and their cronies looted former Yugoslavia's ruins and amassed enormous personal wealth. Mladjan Dinkić, a Serbian economist, has estimated that about U.S. $4.5 billion was diverted into foreign accounts during the early 1990s. The beneficiaries' identities were never established because economic sanctions imposed limits on investigations, but a banker in whom Milošević placed great trust appears to have been at the heart of the matter. Borka Vučić managed the Cyprus branch of Beobanka during Yugoslavia's breakup and worked closely with members of the Serbian government. Her signature was purportedly worth $1,500,000, and there is little doubt that the funds were diverted through her.

As far as anyone has yet been able to determine, the Miloševics did not personally benefit from the embezzlements. They did, however, purchase their home in Belgrade's prime location at a fraction of its value and subsequently had a complete renovation done at the government's expense. Furthermore, they never denied a report in the Greek press which claimed that they had purchased a villa near Athens for over $2 million, and both Slobodan's collected speeches and Mirjana's many books were additional sources of income at a time when the great majority of Serbs could barely afford to purchase a book.

The Miloševics have been known to quarrel, but by and large their quarrels aren't the usual domestic spats regarding children, money, or romantic slights, but are over political appointments and whom they can otherwise trust. Again and again Milošević has yielded to his wife, and anyone who failed to enter into her good graces has suffered, beginning with Ivan Stambolić, who seriously misjudged her influence. She erected barriers between her husband and anyone she didn't like, and he was often forced to meet with his associates behind her back.

No Serbian party had fewer members but more influence than Marković's YUL. It had virtually no following among the electorate, only among government officials. United with other parties representing the non-socialist left, members of YUL were candidates in the 1993 elections and didn't even obtain 1 per cent of the vote.

Everything Marković ever wrote, uttered, or did was covered as though she were a head of state. Industrial labourers who had been on strike for over a year once appealed to her: "We know your word is sufficient to protect what the workforce has been building for forty-three years, and we know you will speak out." Thanks to her marital position, Marković was for years the most powerful Serbian woman ever, far more powerful than anyone merely elected to office. She was responsible for having terminated the careers of countless politicians, and ministerial and diplomatic appointments all became subject to her approval. She has denied her influence, saying that if her opinions seemed influential at times, it didn't mean that she conspired to get her way. What it did mean, she maintained, was that she was able to "see things clearly" and that "events" that coincided with her wishes "merely vindicated" her insight.

Milošević also denied her influence, and once told a reporter from the *Washington Post* that although his wife was "very involved in politics, she never tried to influence" him. But too many policies coincided with her views, and the public, convinced that she was his greatest burden, made her a primary target of ridicule and scorn. Even Bishop Atanasije, one of the leaders of the Serb Orthodox Church in Bosnia, has denounced her, calling her an "evil psychopath."

Pictures of Marković adorned Milošević's office and private quarters. Female figures predominated in paintings in their home, and apparently in their bedroom there hangs a painting of an attractive woman wielding a blood-soaked knife. Jokes about Milošević have focused on his wife's dominance, such as the time they ran out of gas during sanctions and Marković was able to persuade an attendant to fill their tank. "Who's he?" asked Milošević. "My first love," Marković replied. "Had you married him you'd now be a gas-station attendant's wife," he said. "No," she replied, "had I married him, he'd now be the president." Milošević didn't mind such jokes, nor did he demonstrate any discomfort with being taken for his wife's subordinate. He cared more that people regarded her highly than he did that they regarded him highly – rather unusual for a man who believes he is superior to everyone else. But she is his greatest love, his inspiration, and guiding light, and he would do anything for her.

However, as much as Mirjana Marković's ambitions appeared boundless and she was allowed to do whatever she wished, she has always known that she was powerless without Milošević. Nothing that happened in Serbia happened without his approval, and everyone readily accepted his supremacy, including his wife, who could only realize her ambitions through him. She rarely appealed to his authority, preferring to imply that he, obsessed by her "beauty, intelligence, and devotion," always stood behind her. Her wishes thus became his, and she was the only person to whom he submitted. Perhaps not altogether in jest, she once said there would be hell to pay if his devotion to her slackened. However, none of the policies that plagued Serbia for over a decade were implemented against his will. Milošević and Marković were partners and will remain partners until the end. What end awaits them still remains to be seen.

Index